'In this wonderful book, John ___ the many questions Jesus aske ___ questions are one of the mc ___ ... ... or the Gospel accounts – he never makes a statement or gives an answer when he can ask a question instead. Through imaginative storytelling and reflective commentary, this book draws you into twenty of Jesus' most important questions, which ring as true today as ever they did. I loved it and think you will too.'
Dr Paula Gooder, Canon Chancellor, St Paul's Cathedral

'Unusually honest . . . superbly well focused.'
Rowan Williams on *God Lost and Found*

'A very good book by an exceptional leader . . . accessible, encouraging and fun with a steel core that takes one back to the face of Christ and the realities of Christian discipleship.'
Justin Welby on *Living Faithfully*

'With his usual wisdom and good humour, John Pritchard writes for anyone and everyone curious about the varied work of ministry. This book will refresh and illuminate your perspective . . .'
Helen-Ann Hartley, Bishop of Ripon, on *Handbook of Christian Ministry*

'A true genius in spiritual writing . . .'
Martyn Percy, Dean of Christ Church, on *Something More*

John Pritchard was Bishop of Oxford until his retirement. He was formerly Bishop of Jarrow and, before that, Archdeacon of Canterbury. He has served in parishes in Birmingham and Taunton and was Warden of Cranmer Hall, Durham. Other books by the author include *God Lost and Found* (SPCK, 2010), *Ten: Why Christianity makes sense* (SPCK, 2014) and *Five Events that Made Christianity* (SPCK, 2018).

TWENTY QUESTIONS JESUS ASKED

And how they speak to us today

John Pritchard

First published in Great Britain in 2022

Society for Promoting Christian Knowledge
36 Causton Street
London SW1P 4ST
www.spck.org.uk

British Library Cataloguing-in-Publication Data
A catalogue record for this book is available from the British Library

ISBN 978-0-281-08564-4
eBook ISBN 978-0-281-08565-1

Typeset by Fakenham Prepress Solutions, Fakenham, Norfolk NR21 8NL
First printed in Great Britain by Ashford Colour Press
Subsequently digitally printed in Great Britain

eBook by Fakenham Prepress Solutions, Fakenham, Norfolk NR21 8NL

Produced on paper from sustainable forests

Printed and bound in Great Britain by Clays Ltd, Elcograf S.p.A.

For Alison Barr, Gordon Oliver and Michael Irving

Contents

Contents

A word at the beginning

Someone once asked me, 'Is there something you've done that crystallizes your sense of who you are?'

It was an intriguing question. Was there something I'd done that summed up who I was and what I valued? My instinctive answer was that I once trekked to the basecamp of Annapurna in the Himalayas. It felt both adventurous and yet reasonably safe, so it said something about me as a cautious wanderer, an earth-bound romantic, a safety-first explorer. I like a whiff of risk, but I still want my hot chocolate at night. I was interested that this was the experience I chose; why was that?

The right question, put in the right way, at the right time, can open up fascinating layers of self-discovery. You're having coffee with a friend, or maybe it's at the mellow end of the day so it's a glass of wine instead, and one of you asks, 'What do you think really drives you in life? Is it achievements, security, esteem or what?' Suddenly the conversation moves a layer or two deeper. It becomes richer and more rewarding than before.

You're on a country walk with a friend and conversation is flowing easily. Your companion asks, 'What's the most challenging thing that you're facing at present?' or 'What's saving your life at the moment, giving you real pleasure?' Your priest or minister asks you, 'Do you ever think what you'd like as your epitaph?' Your homegroup leader asks, 'What figure in the Bible do you most identify with?' or simply, 'Where have you seen God at work this week?'

The point of these questions is that they open up a different kind of conversation. They invite exploration, they open a window, they disturb the peace, they awaken a dream. They might even start an avalanche. I once asked a busy mum, 'What do you do on Sunday mornings?' She's now ordained.

A word at the beginning

In a far distant incarnation, I was a diocesan youth officer and well established in my Superman phase. I crunched up problems for breakfast, had six bright ideas before lunch and had designed a new youth strategy by dinnertime. It was non-stop action; you couldn't expect me to pray as well! Then I went to a youth officers' conference and a monk asked us, 'How much time do you spend each day in silence?' Bullseye! Exactly what I didn't do, and exactly what I needed. The question sank into my soul and my love affair with silence began.

Offering the right question is a well-practised art in society today. You hear it when an interviewer chases a politician on a morning news programme. You hear it when the host on *Desert Island Discs* teases out eight slices of a life story between records. A counsellor asks careful questions to help a client work her way through a time when the sky fell in. A spiritual director asks acute questions to help someone open up new horizons in his faith.

Sometimes a question might even arrive without any obvious origin. In a famous passage from his book *Markings*, Dag Hammarskjöld, the first Secretary-General of the United Nations, wrote, 'I don't know who – or what – put the question. I don't know when it was put. I don't even remember answering. But at some moment I did answer "yes" to Someone – or Something – and from that hour I was certain that existence is meaningful and that therefore my life, in self-surrender, had a goal.'[1]

Jesus was brilliant at asking the right questions, the sort that opened up new spiritual space and helped people to listen to whispers and hopes from deep within themselves. We tend to think that Jesus was always in 'transmit' mode, always preaching and teaching and sharing the good news of the kingdom. In fact, his method was very often to drop a seemingly innocent question into an encounter, then wait to see what happened. He wasn't looking for 'yes' or 'no' binary answers; he was inviting people into participation and exploration.

Sometimes the question was an invitation: 'What do you want me to do for you?' Sometimes it was a challenge: 'Why are you afraid?' Sometimes it was to lift people up and release them: 'Has no one condemned you?' Sometimes it was to forgive them: 'Simon, do you love me?' Always, though, the question created spiritual space for individuals to explore something about themselves and about God. That space was where new discoveries could be made, where God could be glimpsed wearing new clothes.

Once you notice them, you find Jesus asking scores of questions. The Gospels are peppered with them. Some are rhetorical, so Jesus isn't really expecting an answer: 'What is the kingdom of God like?' *Listen – I'm going to tell you.* Some are aggressive: 'You faithless generation, how much longer must I be with you?' Usually, however, they challenge those Jesus is talking with and make them stop and think how best to answer. Jesus' questions can often be taken at several different levels so, beneath the surface level, he may be inviting others to reassess a significant part of their lives. Even if they answer the question quickly, they're probably instinctively identifying the core issue they're facing. So when Jesus asks the demoniac, 'What's your name?' the man replies that his name is Legion, and recognizes that there's a whole crowd of personalities inside him tearing him apart. He needs to find himself again and be reintegrated into a single personality with a clear identity.

What I especially love about Jesus' questions is that, time and again, I find they have a lasting resonance for us in the present. They disturb, excite and scratch somewhere inside us today as well. They are not tied to the time in which they were originally asked so can still open up a deep level of reflection on the way we live and try to follow Jesus. In other words, these penetrating questions expose new possibilities of life, new avenues of thought and the prospect of personal change. 'What are you looking for?' 'What do you want me to do for you?' 'Are you asleep?' 'Do you love me?' Although these questions, and many others, were asked originally in a very different context from our own, they have an arresting simplicity and a direct relevance to the lives of most of us.

I was 19 when I seriously faced Jesus' question, 'Who do you say that I am?' It was such an innocent question, but so challenging when I realized that I had to answer it properly rather than simply note it as a subject for discussion. Answering that question undermined what I thought I knew about the Christian faith, but it offered a whole new vista of possibilities. I gave an answer that caused my life to swerve in a whole new direction.

What I've tried to do in the chapters that follow is to take 20 of the questions that Jesus asked and handle them in two ways. First, I've told the stories in an Ignatian style, so that we use our senses to enter the narrative; it's sometimes described as using the 'baptized imagination'. In doing so, I've gone beyond the bare words of the biblical text, but I hope that I've done so responsibly. I'm trying to reimagine the impact that the stories would have had when they were first heard. Second, I've gone on to apply the same question that Jesus asked *then* to issues of faith and discipleship *now*. I've tried to follow the spirit of the question, to see where it leads us in our own journeys of faith, both personally and as a church. At the end of the exploration, I've offered some further questions and suggested ways to pray that can be used individually or as a group, for both intercession (A) and a more reflective, contemplative style of prayer (B).

The biggest question of all, of course, is simply Jesus himself. His life, death and new life puts a question mark against our choices, values and priorities. What do we make of his extraordinary teaching in the Sermon on the Mount about a kingdom that seems so upside down we can hardly get our heads around it? What do we make of the cross and the terrible image of a crucified God? What new worlds might we celebrate because of the way life came racing back in the resurrection?

Jesus' own clincher of a question was, 'Who do you say that I am?' Millions of Christians have found that, because of the answer faith gives to this question, everything else begins to fall into place. Jesus always stands before us as the great, compelling enigma who invites a response from every generation, in every age, in every place.

Jesus is God's question. And Jesus is God's answer.

1

'What are you looking for?'
John 1.38 (35–42)

My name is Andrew. I'm 19. I live with my family in Bethsaida, at the north end of the Sea of Galilee. We look right down the length of the lake, and if that isn't a foretaste of heaven, I don't know what is.

We're fishermen in our family. My brother Simon and I should take over the family business eventually. They say that there are more than 200 fishing boats on the Sea of Galilee. That's a lot, but most of us make a decent living, as do James and John with their father Zebedee down in Capernaum by the sea itself. John's a special friend of mine.

He and I have come to know another John recently, the one who's made quite a name for himself by baptizing lots of people in the Jordan. He has really made us stop and think. He's a complete one off. His main message is clear: 'Repent. Turn away from all the rubbish you're doing. And do it now. Get ready for God's arrival and clear a straight path for him.' He tells it straight, no question. Mind you, his dress sense is off the wall. We don't think much of his diet either.

Lately, John has been talking more and more about his cousin Jesus, saying that Jesus is way more important than him. John only baptizes with water (which he does, with such vast quantities of water you're not sure you'll get out alive), but Jesus, he says, baptizes with the Holy Spirit, whatever that means.

Anyway, there we were, chatting with John, and Jesus wandered by. The temptation was too much. My friend John and I excused ourselves as well as we could and hurried off after Jesus.

We wanted to tag along for a while and see why the Baptizer rates him so highly.

Jesus turned to see who was following him, and that's when we got our first glimpse of what's special about him. It wasn't what he looked like particularly. Slightly above medium height, dark complexion, healthy Galilean face – you know the sort of thing. His eyes were certainly memorable, I'll say that – alive, engaging, challenging, even a hint of mischief.

But it was something else that halted us in our tracks. How do you describe someone who kind of 'overflows' the space he's in? My brother Simon is a big personality, but this man is big in a different way. There's a kind of fire inside him, if that makes sense. He has a presence you can't ignore. He sort of hums with life.

Then he asked us a question, and it was pretty direct. 'What are you looking for?' he asked. As blunt as that.

Now, we could have answered that question in a number of ways. 'We want to know why John thinks you're a bit special.' 'We're young men – we're looking for people like you who are a bit different.' 'We want a story to tell when we get home tonight.' But somehow it felt like Jesus was asking us a bigger question than that. What are we looking for? Well, what *are* we looking for? What's going to satisfy our young men's dreams?

We stammered some kind of reply, a question about where he was staying. I suppose, if we're honest, we just wanted to find out more about him. He smiled and said, 'Why not come and see?'

So there we were, spending most of the day with him, listening, asking ridiculous questions, watching how he does things, seeing how easily he talks with people. And I found myself more and more in awe of him. What he says makes so much sense. He seems to know exactly what he's talking about, and has the authority to say it. He's not arrogant, though. He talks about God like he knows him personally. And he talks about us and the people in the villages as if he's known us all his life. It's astonishing.

It was getting near four o'clock and suddenly I felt weary. I don't know about John, but I felt sort of full up, like I couldn't hold any more, but I was bursting to tell Simon about this man. Simon has never been the most tactful member of the family, but he's a born leader and I love him. He speaks when others aren't sure what to say; he acts when others hold back; he's strong and brave, and as honest as the day is long. I share everything with him, so now I simply *had* to share my discovery of Jesus.

I dug him out from behind the house, doing some chores. Maybe I was a bit over the top, but I found myself saying, 'Simon, we've found the Messiah!' The Messiah is the person we believe will come as God's anointed leader, the one who'll win back our land and give us the justice and peace we long for. In a sense, we Jews are always looking out for the Messiah, so it's a pretty big claim I was making here, but Simon could see I was serious, that something big had happened.

I tugged Simon along but, to be honest, he didn't resist. We got down to Capernaum just as Jesus was about to have supper, but he stood up to greet us. He looked at Simon with those deep, searching eyes of his. Then he smiled. 'So you're Simon, are you?' he said. 'I think we'll call you Cephas. Is that OK?' That's like saying he's a stone or a rock or something. You could see that Simon was a bit puzzled, but chuffed as well, as Jesus was saying Simon is strong and reliable, a leader. How does Jesus know?

We stayed for a while, long enough for me to see that Simon was also getting hooked by the indefinable something that drew me in earlier. Jesus talked about a kingdom unlike anything we've ever known – but that, somehow, at the same time, we've always known about. He told stories, he made jokes, he asked questions, he made sense.

Simon and I left Capernaum and, as we wandered back up the dark track to Bethsaida, we were in a kind of excited bubble, remembering, swapping impressions. What are we going to do with all this? One thing I'm sure of: we'll have to go and find Jesus again tomorrow. I don't think Dad will mind us missing work for a bit.

There's a part of me still turning over that first question Jesus asked John and me: 'What are you looking for?' So deceptively simple. So loaded – or am I overcomplicating things? What *am* I looking for?

• • •

How would you answer that question? You might like to journal an answer later on.

When Rassie Erasmus took over as Head Coach of the South African rugby union team in 2018, he changed 13 of the 15 players in the starting line-up. He needed to put together a new team and, a little over a year later, that team won the World Cup. It was bold and brilliant.

Jesus needed to create a new team, too, for the daunting task he had ahead and, in John chapter 1, we see its members being gathered. We're told about Andrew, and a friend who was possibly John or 'the one whom Jesus loved' (John 13.23). Then Andrew's brother, Simon, joined the team, and John's brother James. Then Philip and Nathanael. It was coming together.

Were these young men choosing Jesus or was Jesus choosing them? Both of course, but you get the sense, in this gathering of friends, that Jesus isn't coercing them; rather, he's creating space for them to respond. Jesus said to the two friends, 'Come and see.' Philip found himself saying the same thing to Nathanael: 'Come and see.' In other words, come and see for yourself; you be the judge of whether or not you want to sign up. It must always be the case in discipleship, both then and now, that we're simply invited to come and see, to explore the fit, to encounter the person rather than the theory. Christianity may sound like a good idea, but it can only be proven by coming face to face with Jesus.

Let's imagine that Jesus is asking us the same deceptively simple question noted above: 'What are you looking for?' What would we say?

It's been said that the two most important days of our lives are the day we are born and the day we find out why – what we've actually been looking for. We can spend a long time puzzling over that second one. In Joanna Cannon's book *Three Things about Elsie*, the central figure and narrator, Florence, is living in sheltered accommodation. One day she says this:

'I sometimes wonder what the point of me was. "Does God have a plan, and where does he see me fitting into it?" I asked the vicar once. "We each have a role to play, Miss Claybourne," he said. "Jesus loves everyone." "I'm sure he does," I said, "But love isn't enough, is it? You have to have some kind of purpose. I was wondering what mine might have been?"

'I looked at him. I thought he might give me an interesting answer. Something comfortable and reassuring. But he just checked his watch and started talking to Mrs. Honeyman about harvest festivals. So even the vicar doesn't know why I'm here. "There has to be a reason, though, doesn't there," I said once. "Or have I spent the last eighty-four years just sitting in the audience?" It makes you wonder, though. It makes you wonder if you did have a purpose, but it floated past you one day, and you just didn't think to flag it down.'[2]

What are we looking for? What's the purpose of our lives that makes them meaningful? Without an answer to Jesus' question we can be left wallowing in insecurity and compromise, making up a narrative about ourselves that might fool others, but will never convince us in the quiet watches of the night.

Alfred Nobel became rich as a consequence of inventing dynamite. In 1888 he had the unfortunate experience of reading his own obituary in a French newspaper, because his brother had died and the paper got them mixed up. Alfred read that he was considered a 'merchant of death'. It was a shock. Was that what he wanted to be remembered for? Was that his purpose in life? Perhaps it was that experience which led Alfred to stipulate in his will that his fortune was to be used for what we now know as the Nobel prizes, which are awarded to those who have done their best for humanity in the fields of medicine, literature, the sciences, peace and so on.

Actress Nicole Kidman said that it was winning an Oscar in 2002 which made her realize how empty her life really was. It led to the renewal of her Catholic faith.

'What are you looking for?'

The disciples found the purpose of their lives in following Jesus to his death, and theirs. Christians have found something similar, if usually less dramatic. The confusing thing is that, in the West, most people have most of what they need for most of their lives. Why do we need more? Why do we think that there's something missing? Archbishop Stephen Cottrell answers that question using the image of a musical score. The bass line may be beautiful and seem complete in itself, but when the treble line is played as well, the bass line can still be heard but now in a much more rounded and satisfying way. You never want to play just the one line again. Life in Christ gives us the full musical score.

Jesus gave Simon a new name, Cephas. When we join Jesus' team, we too are given a new name. It is the name of our relationship with Christ, which only we know (Revelation 2.17). The nature of that intimacy is ours alone, and utterly unique. We've found what we've been looking for.

If our *general* purpose is to have that distinctive, unique relationship with Christ, finding our *particular* purpose within that is another exciting journey of discernment. We listen in prayer, not presuming to know the answer too soon; we see where our heart is 'strangely warmed' (in John Wesley's evocative phrase); we talk with friends and beg their honesty; we read the Bible and recognize ideas that keep coming through to us; we read the signs of the times in the practical circumstances of our lives; and we test everything with the plumb line of love.

Your particular purpose might be to start a great charity, but it's more likely to be to support one with time and money. It might be to be a human rights lawyer, but it's more likely to be to pray for one. It might be to be ordained, but it's more likely to be to offer your friendship in a ministry of hospitality. For most of us, Christian vocation isn't found in major changes and grand gestures but in daily faithfulness and long obedience. Spiritual writer Thomas Merton wrote:

If you want to know who I am, don't ask me where I live and what I do, but rather ask me what I am living *for*, and ask me in very small particulars why I'm doing so little about it.

We work out our God-given purpose in very small particulars.

When grace finds us, we need to stop, listen and take good notes. That is what we are here for. What we do for Jesus may seem minor but, as Bishop Philip North said while marking the foreheads of a crowd of teenagers with a cross of glitter, 'Remember you are dust, destined for glory.' Whatever our purpose in Christ, small or great, we are destined for glory.

What are you looking for?

To ponder

- I wonder what the young men were expecting as they took off with Jesus?
- What are you looking for now, at this stage in your life?
- Have you talked with anyone about this? Who would it be if you did?

Prayer

A is for intercession; B is more contemplative.

A Identify and pray for anyone you know who you sense is seeking a new direction or purpose in life. Pray for that purpose to emerge, and for the strength and determination to pursue it.
B Sit with Jesus and let him ask you the question, 'What are you looking for?' Then try to answer the question, replying directly to Jesus. Let that be your prayer

2

'Woman, what concern is that to you and to me?'
John 2.4 (1–12)

I feel a mix of emotions today. Here we are – me, Jesus, his brothers and sisters, and a few of his friends from the lake – at the wedding of two young people, Simon and Esther, whose parents we know well. Everyone knows one another around here. Cana is a nice little village, not far from us in Nazareth, and we've been friends with both families from way back.

Jesus is looking quite handsome, to me at any rate. He's even used a comb for once. But I can't help wondering if he'll ever get married himself. I fear that he might have missed the boat for marriage now. A mother can't help but feel a bit sad about that. He's had lots of friends who were girls, of course; he even had one who I really hoped might be his choice. Rachel. Lovely girl. But I suppose it's always seemed as if Jesus was somehow on a different course. I'm not even sure he knew what it was himself, but he's always been different. And special.

Anyway, it's not his day today. Mind you, it's lovely to see him enjoying himself, going round chatting to everyone. He's good at that – puts people at their ease, always interested in them and listening to their stories. There always seems to be laughter coming from the table he's at. Bless him.

Right now, though, it looks as if something's gone wrong. The boys serving the wine are definitely worried. They're huddled together and looking anxiously towards the steward. They're clearly wondering what to do next.

Oh dear, now I get it – they've run out of wine! That really is a disaster at a wedding. Dear old Sarah and Jacob, they'll have been scrimping and saving for years to have enough money for this wedding. Normally, we have a fairly simple diet in the villages – lots of bread and cheese, olive oil and fruit. For a wedding, though, it's the full works: lamb, chicken, humous, honey, spices, vegetables – every delicacy – and wine, lots of wine. This is going to be so embarrassing for Sarah and Jacob; they'll never live it down.

I know what I have to do straight away. It's not my business, but I must tell Jesus. I don't know what I expect him to do but I'm sure he'll do something. I'll saunter over, trying not to look in a hurry. Jesus senses that I'm there behind him and turns round. Those eyes of his – they see into you every time. I lean towards him and say quietly, 'Jesus, they've run out of wine.' I let it hang in the air.

He looks at me, straight-faced. 'So, Mother, what's that got to do with us, with you and me? In any case, my time hasn't come yet.'

Now, I grant you, that could have sounded a bit harsh, but it wasn't, as it happens. We know what each other is thinking; we have that kind of bond. We understand each other. And I know that nothing will ever separate us except death. My death, I mean, of course.

At the same time, I realize that I have to let him go. He has more on his plate than our family really understands. He's been wonderful at home, of course, running the business with the other boys, especially since dear Joseph died. A bit ago, though, he suddenly said that he had to leave, to go and meet his cousin John down at the Jordan, and he might be away for a while. In fact, he disappeared for a few weeks, said he'd been in the desert to be on his own with God. When he came back, he looked physically worn out to me, but inwardly he seemed strong, and he asked if I'd mind if he went to live down in Capernaum by the lake. I knew better than to object. He knows who he is and what he has to do. He radiates peace and confidence. I can't put my finger on what's so different about him. Anyway, I respect his decision completely.

That doesn't mean I won't worry about him. I worry that the inner freedom he seems to have might get him into trouble some day.

Anyway, we have a more immediate problem on our hands. Wine – or, rather, the lack of it. I smile at him. 'Thank you, Jesus. I'll leave it with you.' I wander off to console poor Sarah, who's clearly in a panic. On the way, I go up to the boys serving the wine and I say to them, 'Don't worry. Just do what Jesus says. I'm sure it'll be all right.'

As I'm talking to Sarah, I keep an eye on what Jesus does. He talks quietly to the serving lads and they hurry off to the big jars standing near the entrance. That's where they get the water to wash the dust off our feet when we arrive, and where we wash our hands before eating. They're big, those jars, they hold about 25 gallons each. Obviously, they're a lot emptier now, as we have used so much water already, but the servers are busy filling them up again for some reason. I can't see how that'll help, but there you go, that's Jesus.

When the jars can't take any more water, Jesus goes over to the boys doing the work, has a word, and they immediately start drawing off some of the water and taking it to the steward. To be honest, I'm not sure David (that's the steward's name) will want any water at this moment. He has a serious crisis on his hands and water isn't the answer. But he takes the cup, drinks, looks at the beaker, drinks some more, then he beams in amazement.

He beckons to Simon, the young bridegroom. I can't resist going over to listen. 'Simon,' he's saying. 'This wine is won-derful. How have you done it? We usually have the best wine early on, while the guests can still recognize how good it is, but you've kept this fabulous wine until now. Congratulations!'

Simon beams. He doesn't mind taking the credit for whatever has gone on here. 'So David, let's get on and serve it,' Simon says proudly.

I love it!

The boys serving the wine go off around the room, carrying their overflowing jugs and filling cups enthusiastically. Even old Uncle Jeremiah's cup, I'm sorry to say, because he's clearly had enough already. Nothing new there, I'm afraid. The volume of noise in the room is getting louder and louder as the wine starts doing its work. I've been calculating and, with 6 water jars, I reckon that we've got 150 gallons of this wonderful wine available. Even for Jesus that's a bit over the top! I know that he loves for people to enjoy themselves, but he certainly didn't learn to celebrate like this at home! There's singing and dancing and laughter and joy all around the room and in the courtyard. The wedding party is clearly back on course.

Later, much later, the party's winding down. Simon and Esther have left. Uncle Jeremiah should have left, but he's still there, half asleep, behind a clutter of empty jugs. The servers are quietly clearing up and Esther's father, Jacob, has his arm round the steward's shoulder, both of them looking very pleased with themselves. Jesus is beginning to gather us up. His brothers and me are going down to Capernaum with his friends for a few days, which will be nice. We'll be able to see where Jesus is living for a while.

Jesus and I find ourselves at the door at the same time. I'm very proud of him, I really am. We catch each other's eye. He winks. 'What has this got to do with you and me, Mother?' he asks, mischievously.

I smile.

Everything, I think. It's got everything to do with him because everything he does is so incredibly generous. I hope he'll always be like that – right to the end.

• • •

In the story of the wedding at Cana, John, the Gospel writer, is putting down a marker, pointing to the glory and generosity of the ministry of Jesus. The question Jesus asks his mother, however, opens up a considerable problem for his modern-day followers. Let's see how the problem evolves.

'Woman, what concern is that to you and to me?'

I was working my way carefully through some caves deep under the Yorkshire Dales. We'd left the light of day and now relied completely on the artificial light of our head torches, which seemed fragile human devices amid the crushing power of this darkness. We crept on. The darkness became more and more oppressive. Natural light seemed a remote memory, although it couldn't have been more than half an hour. We turned a corner and, suddenly, there was a crack in the rock above us and light from the bright world above shot down, like a golden arrow, into our lost world. Relief flooded through me. Light! Glory! It was wonderful.

It's something of that sense of glory which John tries to express in his Gospel. John is always pointing to the glory of Jesus, the Christ, the chosen one: 'The light shines in the darkness . . . and we have seen his glory' (John 1.5, 14); 'Jesus did this, the first of his signs, in Cana of Galilee, and revealed his glory' (John 2.11); 'Father . . . glorify your Son so that the Son may glorify you' (John 17.1). For John, Jesus is the point where divine lightning strikes the earth and the world is scorched with his glory.

Various axes intersect in the person of Jesus: eternity intersects with history, infinity intersects with geography, divinity intersects with humanity.[3] At the point where they all come together, Jesus is displayed as the revelation of God's glory.

I've always loved the miracle at Cana. It speaks of the glory and extravagance of Jesus, the messianic abundance of this 'glorious' figure, who would provide 800 bottles of the finest wine for a village wedding in the backstreets of the Roman Empire. But through that miracle, Jesus gives us an enticing glimpse of the extravagant new wine of the kingdom. The miracle seems to be saying, 'You haven't seen anything yet!' When God's love bursts into our lives, it's literally heaven-sent. We see his glory.

John's Gospel, with the story of Cana at the start, puts us on the boundary between the old world and the new, the crossover point between the beautiful but broken old creation and the glory of the new creation speeding towards us right now. It means that everything Jesus touches springs to life: people are healed, lives are changed, water becomes wine. Because the Word has become flesh,

flesh can become Word in any one of us. We can share that glory. The offer is always on the table for every one of us, just like the wine at the wedding.

What about the question Jesus asked Mary: 'Woman, what concern is that to you and to me?'? Apparently, Jesus was declining to get involved, claiming that it wasn't their responsibility, but Mary knew better – and she knew Jesus knew. She saw that the absence of wine (of 'glory' in John's imagery) was a problem only Jesus could solve, so she told the waiters to do whatever he said. Her answer to the question Jesus asked her was clear: this problem had a lot to do with them.

Isn't it the same for us? We know that we have a problem. If the Word became flesh two thousand years ago and appeared among us full of glory, grace and truth, why today do we see so few signs of this glory, this new creation, breaking into our tired old world, shot through as it is with violence, deceit, greed, corruption and sheer old-fashioned sin – including the damage we're doing to the planet in such a suicidal fashion? How can Christians make such extravagant claims for the new creation and the way that Christ has changed the world? To most of us it looks to be the same mixture as before – beauty and horror, with horror well ahead on points.

'What has this got to do with us?' Well, something's going wrong and we're in the middle of it. The contradiction between what our faith says and what we actually see happening challenges Christians to do some serious repenting, some serious believing and some serious work alongside Jesus. We believe in the transformation of all things by the glory-giving gospel. 'So if anyone is in Christ, there is a new creation,' says St Paul (2 Corinthians 5.17). 'See, I am making all things new,' says the ascended Christ (Revelation 21.5). It takes an awful lot of faith or special pleading, though, to believe all that. Is the water of our present world actually changing into wine? What does it taste like to you, me and the average agnostic? Where is the glory?

Here are some things to put into the balance. In the first place, we shouldn't try to compress an eternal time frame into our own expectation of instant answers. God's chosen processes of evolution by natural selection and the dangerous freedom God gives to us and to all creation show that God's ways are not always our ways, nor is God's time always our time. Slavery was tolerated in Christian society for 1,800 years before it was seen to be incompatible with the gospel. Racism is still having to be rooted out, with long, painful efforts. Nevertheless, we are subject to the slow, steady undertow of grace, through which we eventually find ourselves tumbling into a new world. In time or out of time, God's kingdom will come on earth as it is in heaven. Glory will come through, but it means that we have to repent, believe in and take responsibility for working towards the coming of that kingdom of justice and right relationships. 'What has this got to do with you and me?' A huge amount.

Here's a second thought to consider. With the eyes of faith, we can see how heaven is constantly leaking into earth. Glory is shining through the weeds. We can see it in the million acts of love and generosity that pepper the world every day in, for example, the dedicated work of 30,000 small charities in the UK giving hope to millions, in the 50,000 'communities of grace' (churches) offering God's unqualified love to all and sundry, in the work of hundreds of food banks sadly needed in communities throughout the land, particularly during the COVID-19 pandemic, in the saints we sometimes stumble over and who leave us humbled, in the miraculous progress the world has made in recent years to reduce poverty and widen educational opportunity, in those individual lives that most of us come across where joy reigns and love seems routine. As Jesus said, the kingdom of God is already among us (Luke 17.21). If we open our eyes, the glory of the Lord is shining all around.

'What has this got to do with you and me?' A huge amount. We're called to be part of a church that's hard at work changing water into wine.

In spite of all this, it can still seem that the advance of the kingdom is impossibly slow. The glory of the new creation seems sparse and patchy, but look at it this way: think of a tiny stream, starting high up in the mountains. It bounces its way playfully down the mountainside until it hits a build-up of stones and foliage blocking its path. The stream isn't put off. It finds a way round, over or through the blockage, and continues on its cheerful way. Further down, the stream is joined by other streams feeding in from the sides. Fuller now, it continues down the mountainside until it hits another more serious blockage of rocks, tree roots and other detritus. The stream still isn't put off. It finds a way round, over or through the blockage, and continues on its way downhill. Lower down, it's become quite a torrent, pouring along joyfully, until it meets a landslip. The stream still isn't put off. You get the point. Nothing can hold up the irresistible energy of the stream. At the bottom of the valley, it joins the great river, making its way inexorably to the sea, growing in strength and beauty until, eventually, it flows majestically into the ocean.

So it is with God's loving purpose. Nothing can stop its flow. God is patient, perseveres and, ultimately, is irresistible. The divine Lover may seem to be as vulnerable as the stream, but his love is never defeated because it's inexhaustible. The kingdom is on its way, but we have to align ourselves with the divine purpose and play our part in clearing a passage for the stream to flow and the kingdom to come.

'What has this got to do with you and me?' asked Jesus. The answer is, 'A huge amount.' We have much to repent of in the way things are in the world, much to believe in if we're to take seriously the message of the new creation, and much to do alongside Jesus in laying the foundations of the kingdom. God has shown his glory to be inexhaustible, and all things are transformed in his hands because, eventually, Love will change everything. But this is a huge task, and Jesus rightly asks us if it has anything to do with us. We answer by committing ourselves to preparing the way of the kingdom and doing so daily, in actions large and small.

This is a joint operation. Jesus is in charge, but he needs us on his team.

To ponder

- Does John's word 'glory' resonate with you when you think of Jesus?

- Do you see evidence of a new creation growing around us?
- How, in your own faith, do you hold together the beauty and the horror of life?

Prayer

A is for intercession; B is more contemplative.

A Remember and give thanks for those places where, in the last few days, you've glimpsed glory 'shining through the weeds'. Don't rush, take your time and pray for a greater awareness and recognition of those glimpses. In a group, you could share such experiences before praying.

B Think of a person, place or situation that's on your heart, for whatever reason, and see that person, place or situation bathed in the glory of God, transfigured, healed. Hold that vision for as long as seems good and right.

3

'Are you a teacher of Israel, and yet you do not understand these things?' John 3.10 (1–16)

The day is cooling down as I slip out of the house quietly. The evening air envelops me like warm silk. I try not to look furtive but, equally, I really don't want to be seen as I set off for the other side of the city.

My name is Nicodemus. I'm a member of the Sanhedrin and some have seen me as a bit of a rising star. That's nonsense, of course, especially as I'm feeling increasingly out of step with my fellow Pharisees. Only Joseph, my friend from Arimathea, seems to feel like I do. Together we make up the entirety of the Sanhedrin's loyal opposition.

And I'm about to make the situation worse.

I pretend that I'm not keeping in the shadows of the old stone buildings but, to be honest, I am. I'm thinking, 'Is this wise?', but it's becoming increasingly obvious to my colleagues that I believe we're heading in the wrong direction. We're promoting a backward-looking understanding of the law, and defending it with increasing ferocity. I want so much more for our religion. The law is supposed to set us free, not tie us up in knots. We might be singing the right song but we're singing it to yesterday's tune.

Then there's this young teacher who seems to get it. Everyone says that he sings the song of our faith beautifully – so beautifully, in fact, that some of my colleagues are muttering that he's dangerous and has to be stopped, even got rid of. How ridiculous! I want to listen to this young man, talk with him, find out why he's so popular.

'Are you a teacher of Israel, and yet you do not understand these things?'

That's why I'm on my way now, as the sun fades and the day slides into night. I want to hear him out, perhaps even see what I'm missing.

I turn left down an alleyway, then right. I don't know this part of the city very well. I feel a bit self-conscious, dressed as I am in my rather elegant day robes (I didn't have time to change). When I get to the address I've been given, it's almost as if he's waiting for me. He greets me with a smile. 'You must be Nicodemus. Welcome.'

He sits us both down in the quiet courtyard as the evening settles around us. He pours us some wine. He's not in a hurry to find out why I've come; he's giving me space. Instead, I stumble in without any subtlety at all. 'Rabbi' – I want to be gracious – 'we know that you're a teacher who's come from God. You couldn't be doing these extraordinary things otherwise.'

I pause. I'm not sure where I'm going with this. Why didn't I think it out properly beforehand? Anyway, I don't have time to frame a question because Jesus (that's his name) comes straight in with something that takes me completely by surprise. 'You know, don't you, that you can't see God's kingdom without being born from above?' I'm wrong-footed straight away – what on earth does he mean by that?

I stammer out the first thing that comes into my head. 'Surely you're not suggesting that we can enter our mother's womb a second time and be born again, are you?' It sounds pretty silly even as I say it. I take a quick gulp of wine to cover my embarrassment.

'No, Nicodemus; it's a figure of speech. I'm saying that if we're going to be part of the kingdom that God's designed for us, we have to be born not only in an ordinary human way but also in a spiritual way, with the life-giving Spirit of God himself. That's what I mean by "from above". It's that experience which raises our faith from rules and rituals to what God truly wants – for us to enjoy his presence, his life in us, with all that flows from this intimacy, such as love, peace, justice and so much more.'

I like what I'm hearing but he's going too fast for me. I try to look intelligent.

'Are you a teacher of Israel, and yet you do not understand these things?'

'Come on, Nicodemus,' he grins. 'Try this. The breeze is gentle tonight, isn't it? But remember the other day, when the wind blew us all over the place? The wind blows when and where it likes. We can't tell it what to do. It's like that when we let the Spirit of God loose in our lives. It's wonderful, crazy, unpredictable, glorious! Don't you see? I know you do.'

I don't.

But I'm trying. 'How can that happen?' I ask lamely.

Then Jesus asks me a question that, if I'm honest, wounds me. 'Are you one of our esteemed teachers and you don't understand these basic things?' I don't think he means it maliciously; he's really simply being mischievous, but with a proper challenge beneath the playfulness. Anyway, the question hits me in both the head and the heart. All this great wisdom we Pharisees have accumulated over years of study, yet have we missed the centre of it all?

Of course, that's just what I've been suspecting. Which is why I'm here.

Fortunately, he doesn't press me for an embarrassed answer. He carries on helping me to see my religion through fresh eyes. He talks about what he believes is his part in God's work. He's also very keen to get across that God doesn't want to condemn the world through our religion. He's not a punishing parent, not an unpredictable tyrant. Rather, he wants to save the world from its troubles – to give us what he calls 'abundance' in our experience of life.

We talk on into the night. Nibbles are brought, humous and olives. More wine. I'm not sure which is more intoxicating – the wine or the wisdom that flows from this impressive young man. When I finally stagger out into the street, I'm dizzy from both. I wonder what to do with all these ideas buzzing through my head. I know one thing, though – I'm going to look out for Jesus. I may be able to help him in some way. He's certainly helped me tonight.

In the meantime, I'm going to have to work hard on that question he put to me in the middle of our conversation: 'Are you one of our esteemed teachers of Israel and you don't understand these basic things?'

'Are you a teacher of Israel, and yet you do not understand these things?'

As I wander back through the dark streets, it feels like I'm a child, just at the beginning.

• • •

You may not be a qualified teacher but the lives of all of us involve 'teaching' the faith every day. It's in how we do ordinary things, and how we live, love and heal the bit of the world we occupy with others. So the question Jesus asked Nicodemus could well be addressed to us as well. Do we understand the things at the core of our faith or have we done as Nicodemus did and gained much information and knowledge, but at the expense of what's really the heart of the matter? There's a case to be made that we've often missed the core of the faith by an inch that's ended up being a mile.

Of course, information and knowledge are important. I used to run a theological college, so I can hardly be uninterested in teaching the central beliefs of Christianity. I still read about the faith incessantly. I'm fascinated by the issues that make up a coherent and persuasive system of belief. This, though, is where the missing inch comes in. Is the Christian faith, essentially, to be found in a series of beliefs, doctrines and confessional statements or is it a new relationship with God that leads to the practice of love and the pursuit of justice? I read Jesus here as teaching his listeners not a system of belief but, rather, an alternative wisdom, a way to love God and neighbour from a new source.

He was teaching about a kingdom that had already arrived and encouraging his followers to live in the radical 'upside downness' of that kingdom. He outlined this world in the Sermon on the Mount, where he taught that everything – from money and relationships to conflict and prayer – should be done in a different way. It should not come from commands and prohibitions but from the reality of a new relationship with God.

American writer Brian McLaren makes a clear proposal:

What would it mean for Christians to rediscover their faith not as a problematic system of beliefs, but as a just and generous way of life, rooted in contemplation and expressed in compassion? Could Christians migrate from defining their faith as a system of beliefs to expressing it as a loving way of life?[4]

Such a proposal isn't new. Poet Samuel Taylor Coleridge wrote in 1884, 'Christianity is not a theory or a speculation but a life; not a philosophy of life, but a life and a living process . . . Try it.'[5]

Again, this is not being anti-intellectual. I'm thrilled when I find people are engaging in theology or biblical studies and being excited by it. Again and again, I've found all that's necessary for this to happen is for someone's appetite to be whetted, and then they find that the pursuit of understanding in a taster course or training for some form of ministry is completely absorbing and life-changing. We can be deeply energized by the process of learning.

That said, the satisfaction of this hunger usually rests on a deeper need which has, in some way, been met or glimpsed or sought already, and that's the need for some form of encounter with God. It's this reality that the soul craves, and its practical outworking in the mess and muddle of ordinary life. Are these the things that we teach and learn – how to encounter God and live faithfully in response?

'Are you one of our esteemed teachers of Israel and you don't understand these basic things?'

Obviously, how we encounter God is difficult to teach or learn because it's a mystery lodged in the even greater mystery of God. For some of us it comes in the form of a profound response to the beauty of nature and an awareness of its divine imprint. Some of us experience an unfamiliar stirring of the spirit, a nagging need to look deeper. Others find it in the compelling words of Scripture that warm the heart and stir the will. For others of us again, it comes in a top-to-toe conversion experience that makes everything look different.

Acclaimed American writer Marilynn Robinson says, 'Religion is human behaviour; grace is the love of God.'[6] It's grace that we need to learn and teach; grace that we need to experience as the richest gift of faith. When I finally understood that, when it had finally got through the layers of trust that I still placed in the conventional securities of possessions and personal prestige, it was then that I came to 'the heart of the heart' of the Christian faith. It was all about grace. I was in my thirties before I got there, already ordained for a number of years. It isn't always easy to learn the simplicity that lies at the centre of complexity. I'd previously always majored on understanding. I thought that if people understood the Christian faith properly, they would commit themselves to it. I still want to understand, and for other people to understand. I still think it's of real importance and that we must never sell the faith short intellectually. It can captivate the deepest thinkers and the biggest brains. However, it's not the molten core of faith. Karl Barth, one of those 'biggest brains', was on his way to the United States of America later in life and he was asked how he would summarize the millions of words he had written as a theologian. He said, 'Jesus loves me, this I know, for the Bible tells me so.' Grace, the love of God, received and lived out, is the core of the Christian faith.

New Zealand retreat leader and spiritual director Sue Pickering writes:

It's one of the saddest things to see elderly people who have been exposed to Sunday School or church for most of their lives, still not really knowing that God loves them and is with them. These people form a significant number of our current congregations, and the duty of care we owe them goes far beyond keeping them comfortable with more of the familiar until we take their funerals. We have a responsibility to offer them opportunities for spiritual growth, a chance to have their spiritual needs met, and above all, the comfort of knowing that God is with them all the way home.[7]

'All the way home' is a lovely way of imagining the journey of faith. We end as we began – in the heart of God.

As a teacher of Israel, Nicodemus had all the right motives. He wanted the law to guide and enrich people's lives, but the challenge of Jesus was that he had missed his goal by an inch that became a mile. That could be our problem, too, if we see the Christian faith as a repository of truths rather than a way of transformation.

Do we understand these basic things?

To ponder
- I wonder if you've usually thought of the Christian faith as a set of beliefs or as 'a loving way of life'?
- What does 'encountering God' mean for you?
- How has your understanding of faith changed over time?
- What helps you go deeper in your faith?

Prayer
A is for intercession; B is more contemplative.

A Pray for any people you know (priest, minister, bishop, teacher) who have a responsibility for teaching the faith and helping people to learn and grow. Pray that each has a mind that's constantly being refreshed, and a heart that's set on Christ and the growing maturity of his people.
B Imagine yourself 'sunbathing' in the warmth of God's love. Go outside (in your imagination), lie down and relax; let the sun do the rest. Be aware of the warmth of the sun permeating your whole being. Rest in God.

4

'Why are you afraid?'
Mark 4.40 (35–41)

Yes, I know I've been a fisherman all my life, but I still don't like it when a storm makes me feel like I'm about to be thrown to the fishes.

It started out like any other day, Jesus teaching the crowds that seem to pop up out of nowhere wherever he goes. By late afternoon, he was clearly exhausted. It hadn't helped that he'd been up half the night with a couple who'd lost their son in an accident. He always makes time for people, but now his face was lined with weariness.

We needed to get away. Even Jesus recognized this and it was he who suggested that we go over to the other side of the lake for a bit. It's Gentile territory there, on the eastern shore, and so the people are not really aware of what Jesus has been doing. Everyone thought that it was a good idea. We were all tired from the heat and doing our best to protect Jesus – from himself as much as from the crowds – so we set off in the late afternoon sun, pulling gently on the oars, a light breeze in the sails. Jesus immediately sank into the cushions in the stern and fell asleep.

If only it had stayed like that, nice and calm, as we slowly relaxed after the strain of the day.

At first it was just a squall. We weren't alarmed – we get those on the lake – but soon enough the wind got up and the waves were growing bigger by the minute. Before we knew it, there was a full-scale storm. Waves were swamping the boat and it was being tossed around like a leaf in a waterfall. We hung on to anything that looked like it wouldn't break apart. I looked at my friends, most of them experienced sailors, and we were all looking tense. Verging on panic. We knew this lake and it could be vicious.

I think it was James who said what we were all thinking. He shouted over the roar of the storm. I couldn't really hear him, but I could see what he meant: we must wake Jesus.

I was nearest. I gave his shoulder a shake. Nothing. He was dog tired. I shook him harder. He opened an eye. 'Is there a problem?' he mouthed, the words lost in the howling wind.

Is there a problem?! For heaven's sake. Is Pontius Pilate a Roman tyrant? Of course there was a problem! We were about to drown.

Another deluge of water crashed into me, taking my breath away. I managed to gasp out my complaint: 'Look, Jesus, we're drowning. Don't you care?' I admit I was sharp.

Jesus sat up, holding on to the side of the boat. He looked around, then smiled at us. Smiled! Jesus' timing isn't always great (or perhaps it is). Anyway, he looked across the angry water, then up at the dark sky, with the clouds driving past, and he said firmly and clearly to everything around us, 'Peace! Settle down! Be still.'

That is when it got seriously weird. Immediately – and I mean immediately – I felt calm inside. It was all right. I knew it. A few moments later, I was sure the wind was dropping a bit as well. Three or four minutes after that and the storm was clearly dying away. How did he do that? Did he do that? It was extraordinary. Gingerly, we stood up and shook ourselves down.

Jesus looked at the relief on our faces. He grinned. 'Why are you afraid?' he asked. As if it wasn't obvious.

I love it when he grins. All his attractive personality is packed into that grin. People get so excited about his teaching and healing and all that, but they often forget what good company he is. He's wise, kind, thoughtful, clever and the rest of it, but he's also great fun. Sometimes at our evening mealtimes, we laugh until we ache. He's a great storyteller of course but, more than that, he kind of shines with life, if you know what I mean, and we get caught up in it. We're spellbound.

'Why are you afraid?' He asked that seemingly innocent question with a mischievous grin, but it seemed to me that there was a deeper question lurking behind it. As so often. He seemed to be saying, 'Believe me, you really are safe with me. Maybe not physically, but in all the ways that truly matter.' He seemed to be asking a question, but really it was an invitation, an invitation to trust him very deeply.

I do trust him – or try to. I feel much safer when I'm near him. I'm sure I've got a lot more to learn about trust – it's early days – but I've never felt so secure with anyone else, even with our parents when I was a boy. I felt like that on the water in the storm. Immediately he spoke, I felt calm. It was all right. I knew it. Deep down, everything was all right.

'Why are you afraid?' he asked.

Yes, why was I afraid when I had a friend like that?

• • •

When are you afraid? We may not want to admit it, but it's totally normal to be afraid sometimes. What, though, are we supposed to do with our fears?

There have been two occasions in my life when, for some reason, I allowed myself to be convinced that walking on burning coals was a good idea. The fact that there were two hours of motivational training beforehand didn't eliminate the trepidation entirely. Nor did it escape my notice that there was an ambulance standing by. I'm still here to tell the story, and could even let you know the physics of why it can be safe to walk on coals burning at 1,000 °F (540 °C), but I'm not going to recommend it to anyone with a nervous disposition.

There are some situations where fear is entirely reasonable. Walking on burning coals is one. Being caught in a small boat in a violent storm is another. At the height of the COVID-19 pandemic, millions of people were rightly afraid of leaving their homes, particularly if they were older, had underlying health conditions, and were male (for the record, that was me).

There are, perhaps, two stages to go through when facing our fears in situations like these. The first is to check that the fear we feel is well founded in terms of the facts. That doesn't mean the fear is wrong, because 'fear is fear' for the person experiencing it, but we might be able to relativize its intensity by calling it out, by naming it.

There's a fable about a demon deciding to distract a man hurrying along a road. The demon roared and screamed and vomited, but the man simply raised his hat and walked by. It then tried appearing as a huge snake, spitting venom and blocking the road. The man hit it with a stick and carried on. In desperation, the demon then appeared as a psychopathic murderer, waving an axe and uttering obscenities, but the man just smiled and waved back. The demon was astonished and then came beside the man. 'Tell me, traveller,' it said. 'Why are you not afraid?' 'Oh, but I am,' said the man. 'I'm afraid that if my mind keeps producing this sort of rubbish I won't reach my destination before sunset.'[8]

Some fear can be laid to rest by examining the facts – such as my experience with burning coals and, for a long time, my fear of going to the dentist. It's then possible that we can be lured down from the ledge of imminent disaster we've got stuck on. Our fears might be at least partially allayed.

There is, however, a more important stage in facing our fears. That is when the fear is not only entirely reasonable but also pretty well inevitable, because any normal person would feel the same. My wife and I were in charge of three precious grandchildren while their parents were away briefly. You can imagine our fear when we had to rush the smallest grandchild to hospital with suspected meningitis. Our fear was entirely justified. It wasn't that we needed to be more trusting and improve our prayer life.

A simple piece of wisdom is this: don't be afraid of being afraid. Let it be.

Jesus, however, seems to be offering something more. It was completely understandable that the disciples felt afraid as they were thrown about by the storm. In an argument, the sea always has the last word but, in this case, it was Jesus who had the last word. The word was 'peace'. It was spoken to both the storm and the disciples.

Jesus took his friends to a place beyond fear. It was a place of greater safety, and it was based on being with Jesus.

We might also find that to be a safe place when a situation itself is dire but we discover we have a faith that's equal to it. It's the confidence that comes from 'letting go' into Christ. It means facing the fear, in all its stark reality, looking at it, understanding it, then going through it to the other side. It's like passing through a waterfall and finding ourselves behind the curtain of water, where all is calm, and the ferocity of the water can't affect us. That is the kind of place where we know that nothing 'will be able to separate us from the love of God in Christ Jesus our Lord' (Romans 8.39). In an ultimate sense, we are safe; it's the place of greatest safety.

Martin Luther King Jr was a young black pastor and he had just got out of jail when he received a death threat on the phone: 'Nigger, if you aren't out of this town in three days, we're going to blow your brains out, and blow up your house.' He sat in the kitchen and thought of his loyal wife and newborn daughter asleep upstairs:

I bowed down over that cup of coffee. I prayed a prayer that night. I said, 'Lord, I'm down here trying to do what's right. I think I'm right. I think that the cause we represent is right. But Lord, I must confess that I'm weak now. I'm faltering.'

Understandably, he was afraid, exposed as if in a small boat on a wild sea, like the disciples, but he went on:

'It seemed at that moment that I could hear an inner voice saying to me, "Martin Luther, stand up for righteousness. Stand up for justice. Stand up for truth. And I will be with you, to the end of the world." I heard the voice of Jesus say still to fight on. He promised never to leave me alone. No never alone. Never alone. He promised never to leave me, never to leave me alone.' Three nights later a bomb exploded on the front porch, filling the house with smoke and broken glass, although no one was injured. But King was ready now. He wasn't turning back.[9]

Martin Luther King had entered that place of greater safety. At one level, of course, he was afraid, and he had every reason to be, but, underneath, he had found a peace that couldn't be shaken. The surface of the water might be violently disturbed, but six feet under the waves it was another story.

Finding our way to this place doesn't happen automatically. It may only come with tears and struggle. It's realistic, not magic. When the breakthrough is made, though, there's a calm, a 'peace . . . which surpasses all understanding' (Philippians 4.7). I've seen it in people facing death and dangerous operations. I've seen it on the news in hostages facing immense danger. These are not a different breed of people; they're ordinary people who have found their way to an extraordinary place.

Jesus knew what it was to be afraid. We read that in Gethsemane his fear was so acute, his sweat looked like drops of blood as he agonized with God over what the next day would bring. But he found his way through it and, from then on, he never looked back. That's what I mean by a place of greater safety.

'Why are you afraid?' Jesus asks us.

He has a better place to offer.

To ponder

- What are you afraid of?
- Have you, on some occasions, found that place of greater safety?
- I wonder who you've admired who faced their fears and found a deeper peace?

Prayer

A is for intercession; B is more contemplative.

A Pray for anyone you know who is or may be afraid because of issues of health, relationship, employment, finances. Pray for those near them, that they'll know what to say and do. Perhaps place a glove before a cross or candle and put a stone or hazelnut into the open palm as you pray for each one, the glove representing God holding each person in the palm of his hand.

B   Gently practise the Jesus Prayer ('Lord Jesus Christ, Son of God, have mercy on me, a sinner'), repeating it as often as you like. This can be an especially supportive way of praying in times of anxiety or crisis.

5

'What is your name?'
Mark 5.9 (1–20)

My name is . . . well, it doesn't matter. They say I'm possessed by a demon or something. They must be right – I really don't feel well.

In fact, I'm in pieces, as if there's a battle going on inside me and, whoever wins, I've lost. When things are at their worst, I go completely crazy and start screaming and yelling and running all over the place. I really don't remember afterwards. I wake up aching, with bruises all over my body. Someone must have been hitting me with the stones that lie all over the hillside. Or was I hitting myself? I really don't know who's who any more. Sometimes when I'm feeling calmer, I think of the demons in me as my friends, my companions. They tell me who I am.

The hillside. That's where people try to keep me chained up, but when the demons in me get really angry, they can break those shackles as if they were a daisy chain. They don't like being chained up. They want to be able to wander round the tombs at night and cry at the moon. Sometimes I try to calm them down, but then they shout at me even louder.

Now, this morning, I can see a fishing boat coming into shore from the other side of the lake. I have a nasty feeling about that boat, as if it's bringing danger. My demons feel the same. There's a man in there who spells trouble; I can sense it. There's power around and I don't like it. None of us likes it. We must go down there, to see him off. I leap down the hillside to confront him, all of us screaming and shrieking obscenities.

Why isn't it working? He's just calmly standing there, quietly telling my friends to leave me now, immediately, to return to the land of darkness. I'm shocked. How could I manage without my companions? I find myself on the ground, shouting at the top of my voice, 'What have you got to do with me, Jesus? What have we got in common, you Son of Almighty God? Get away from me! Stop torturing me!' My friends obviously know who he is, even if I don't. I'm beside myself with fear; I'm frothing at the mouth. I'm sick. I'm sick.

I'm silent.

Stillness. I hear birds singing, waves licking the shore.

Then he asks me a question that gets right inside me: 'What's your name?'

For God's sake! What's my name? Which one does he want! I've got names for every day of the week and every week of the year! Which name fits today?

But it's the right question. I find myself saying, 'My name is Legion. There are loads of us.'

Suddenly, I'm tired. Tired like the end of the world. Tired like it's all over.

Summoning our last scraps of energy, we start pleading with him. 'Please, send us into those pigs – those pigs over there at the top of the hill. It's too painful near you. We'll be safe in those pigs. You've got to let us go . . .'

And he does. I feel I huge wrench inside me, tearing me inside out, a flood of pain released. It's terrible and wonderful at the same time. I collapse, exhausted, my body emptied out.

I fall asleep.

When I wake up I've no idea how long I've been out of it. Nearby, the man (I think the demons called him Jesus) is talking quietly with his friends, but lots of other people have arrived too. The word must have got out. I vaguely remember some of those people, as if from another life. They're from the village nearby. I sit up. They're saying something about the pigs they look after, that the pigs have charged down the hill and now they're lost.

That's weird.

I try to work out how I'm feeling. Like spring. Like sunshine on the lake. Like newly washed fields. Like a newborn child dipped in love. It's wonderful. I'm still alone, though. The villagers have seen too much of me and my friends in the past; they keep their distance, occasionally glancing in my direction, as if afraid that I'll suddenly leap up and scream at them.

I won't scream. I'm different now.

I want to go and thank Jesus. In fact, I want to stay with him, where I feel safe. I want to see how he handles that strange power he has, listen to what he says and learn more. What could be better? I've had it here anyway. Too many memories, for both me and the poor locals I've terrorized for so long.

So I stand up, shakily, and stammer out my request. Jesus looks at me kindly, but I can see what he's going to say. 'No, my friend,' he says. 'You must stay here and share with these good people what God has done for you. This is Gentile country, not Jewish. They haven't heard how God is doing something new in our lands, both yours and mine. They need you.'

My heart sinks, but I know he's right. I want to tell people about Jesus.

What is my name? It doesn't really matter. I am one person, and I'm healed.

• • •

In *Alice's Adventures in Wonderland*, the Caterpillar asks Alice who she is, and she says:

> 'I hardly know, sir. At least, I know who I was when I got up this morning, but I think I must have been changed several times since then.'[10]

Most of us, at some time or other, are probably conscious of a number of different personalities jostling for position inside us. When I'm preaching in church or speaking at a conference with my wife present, she might (being the generous person she is) see the experienced teacher, the careful listener, everybody's friend. She must think, 'Where's the grumpy hypochondriac I know at home?' Among my many personalities is a self-absorbed writer, a frustrated traveller, a doting grandfather and a selfish layabout.

'What is your name?' How many personalities do you have, or facets of your personality? Do you like them? What's their story? Crucially, how do you feed them? The ones we feed – the ones to which we give an extra helping of attention or encouragement – are the ones that prosper.

The story of Jesus and the possessed man in Gadara is both well known and strange to many modern ears. Whatever the precise events, it clearly contains truth, but at a number of levels. One of the least important is probably what a camera crew would have focused on. What actually happened to that herd of pigs is not, in a sense, of huge importance to us, although, I freely grant, the owners of those pigs might have felt differently.

The story is about many things. Theologically, it's about the authority of Jesus, specifically the authority of Jesus in Gentile as well as Jewish lands. It gave the early Church a mission imperative to take the gospel beyond the usual boundaries to the ends of the known world. Christians then, as now, are called to inhabit the borderlands and make sure that the gates are all open and the fences are being taken down. The inclusivity of Christianity is a clear characteristic of a faith that even the bleakest attitudes of believers have not been been able to foil, because it's non-negotiable:

There is no longer Jew or Greek, there is no longer slave or free, there is no longer male and female; for all of you are one in Christ Jesus.
(Galatians 3.28)

Personally and spiritually, however, the story is about the power of Jesus to restore a person to his or her own unified identity. The man in the story is asked another of Jesus' deceptively simple questions: 'What is your name?' Jesus recognized that here was a man of many personalities, a lot of them deeply destructive. These were the demons that possessed him. It doesn't much matter how we perceive those demons – as objective entities or as representations of his mental illness. The point is to take them seriously.

The man gives an honest and revealing answer: 'My name is Legion, because there's a whole crowd of us running around in my life.' Emotionally, he was all over the place. He needed to find himself again, to be reintegrated into one, unified personality with a clear, stable identity. That is what Jesus did for him – this frightened, lonely man who lived among the tombs on a hillside surrounded by pigs. He healed him. More than that, he saved him. So now this man sat at Jesus' feet, dazed but free. It started when Jesus came ashore, saw a man in trouble and asked him his name. It was Legion, the curse of the divided self.

What Jesus did for the man he can do for us. It starts when he asks us, 'What is your name?'

One of the most powerful effects of finding a living faith is that it begins to integrate our various personalities into a whole and, hopefully, that 'whole' is the best expression of what it is to be you and me. By having God as the integrating centre of our lives, the different elements all begin to come together, and the personalities within us make friends with one another. We begin the process of becoming whole.

When I went to university, there were various characters rattling round inside me. There was the proto-academic who needed to prove himself when up against stiffer competition, the sportsman who would never be quite good enough at any of his chosen pursuits, the cultural novice who longed to know more, the pseudo-thinker who wanted to be wise, the insecure teenager who wasn't sure how to party, the part-time Christian who wasn't clear about what faith meant. All those characters were spinning around in the complex personal world of me, but nothing really held them together except a pervasive sense of bewilderment and desire. I needed a locking nut at the centre, a hub to integrate and make sense of my various aspirations. I found that locking nut in a faith which was intellectually coherent and emotionally satisfying. With God at the centre, seen through the newly compelling figure of Jesus, everything began to fit into place. There was a sun at the centre of my solar system. There were still many different facets to my life, but they were integrated around a unifying principle: faith.

My journey is echoed in the experiences of many people. We have an abiding need to understand who we are in the scheme of things, and to know that our lives make sense. Without that assurance we may continually feel adrift among the contradictory opinions of others or the illusions of our own inner turmoil. Who am I? What is my name? In old age, composer Igor Stravinsky would call out from his room for the attention of his wife or anyone else in the household. 'What do you need?' they would ask. 'To be reassured of my own existence,' he would reply. Confirmation of that existence would come in the form of a kiss, a hand holding his or the playing of a record. He needed something beyond himself to reassure him of what he perceived to be his own reality.

In our day, Jesus continues to ask us our name, to name our own multitude. We are many, but we're invited to become one whole person, living fully in the love of God. We become one person when we worship one God. We discover that we are most fully ourselves when we most fully belong to God.

At the beginning of 2020, Liverpool's Brazilian striker Roberto Firmino shared an unusual post with his 13 million Instagram followers. It was a video of his baptism. The caption read, 'I give you my failures, and the victories I will give you too. My biggest title is your love, Jesus.' Of all the names and titles we may or may not have, the most significant is that of being a child of God.

There's a story that echoes around in my memory as I ponder these things. An officer in the First World War was looking after a young soldier who had been gassed, blinded and was suffering shell shock. The officer took him behind the lines to a rest camp where the soldiers had set up a boxing ring. Between the bouts of boxing, the officer (George MacLeod, who later founded the Iona Community) led the young soldier into the ring and told the crowd that the soldier had lost his memory and if anybody recognized him, could they please shout out. There was silence. Suddenly the man screamed out, 'Can nobody tell me who I am?' No one could do that.

'What is your name?'

That was the cry of the possessed man among the tombs near Gadara. Fortunately, and wonderfully, he met Jesus, who heard his agonized cry and helped him find out who he was.

It started with a simple question: 'What is your name?'

To ponder

- I wonder how the former 'demoniac' went on to relate to the villagers and the owners of the pigs, and they to him?
- Can you name some of the different facets of your personality, and how integrated they feel to you?
- I wonder if or when you began to feel your life 'coming together' and how it happened?
- What remains to be integrated?

Prayer

A is for intercession; B is more contemplative.

A Pray for anyone you know who's suffering from mental health issues, and for the mental health teams in your area. Pray also for young people known to you who are subject to much peer and cultural pressure around issues of body image and self-worth.

B Pray for anyone you know who has your first name! As you breathe in, let God say to you, '[Your name], I love you.' As you breathe out, say to God, 'Lord, I love you.' Repeat as many times as feels right . . . then rest in God.

6

'Who touched my clothes?'
Mark 5.30 (21–40)

It feels like my last chance. Twelve years of this interminable bleeding. I've tried everything, believe me. I had money once – did you know that? No more. It's all gone on useless doctors. It's not their fault, of course, but whose fault is it, then? Is it mine?

One thing I do know: it's disgusting. Finding rags, washing rags, disposing of rags – my life is all about rags. Yet the bleeding goes on. It never seems to end. It's utterly exhausting. It feels like my life is being washed away all the time. I wonder how long my wretched body can keep going.

I hate my body.

Of course, this bleeding means that I'm always unclean, impure, untouchable. My husband was pretty clear about that and he's long gone. I'm sure the other women in the village know what's going on. I don't tell them outright, of course, but sometimes I hear it on the street: 'There's the dirty woman.'

Who am I? I'm the woman who bleeds.

Then this miracle man arrived. At least, that's what I've heard about him. People are healed . . . and he preaches like an angel. As I said, it could be my last chance. I know it's getting worse – I'm wiped out most of the time now. At the same time, if I go up to him and ask for his help, everyone will know what's been going on and it'll be all over the village before nightfall. The shame, the shame.

Should I go and find him? Yes? No?

I must.

I watch for his arrival, but when I spot him, he's surrounded, as you'd expect, by crowds of eager people. These are my neighbours, people who might have been friends in my former life. It's pretty chaotic. People are pressing in close, his friends trying to make a path for him. I hear something about Jairus, one of the synagogue leaders, needing help. I think, if I can wriggle my way through these hot, excited bodies, maybe I can get close enough just to touch him. I've been told that sometimes it's all that's needed with these miracle people. Just a touch. Then I'll slip out of the crowd without anyone knowing I've been there. But I'll be well. Won't I? Anyway, I've tried everything else.

Yes, I know I shouldn't be doing this, getting in among all these people, what with me being unclean and all that. It offends the precious purity codes they go on about in the synagogue (another place I can't go), but I'm desperate, so I'm going into that crowd.

My heart is pounding. Just a touch, just a touch . . . I'm reaching out – and missing. I try again – I miss again. There are bodies surging around him. It's all pushing and shoving and me trying to find a way through . . . I don't dare to look at the people around me; they might recognize me and see what I'm doing. I'm only looking at that one person, and how to get near him. Just a touch . . . I think I can reach the back of his robe . . . just a touch . . .

Got it!

Wow! What *have* I got? I feel something rushing through me. I feel a power, a cleansing, a feeling like summer, like fresh water on a hot day. I know that something has definitely changed inside me! Is this real? Is this me? Is this paradise? I'm standing in the marketplace, dazed, as the crowd surges past me. I know that my bleeding has stopped.

Then suddenly, as fast as it happened a moment ago, it all goes horribly wrong and I come down to earth with a bang. He's stopped too, and he's looking around. 'Who touched my clothes?' he says.

Oh no, please don't. Please don't show me up. Please don't make me an exhibit, 'the woman who used to bleed'. Please just give me a smile (he has a lovely smile) and carry on, to help Jairus with whatever his problem is. There's no need for this public humiliation.

But he's still standing there, waiting. Please don't do this. Why is it necessary? Please don't add to my shame . . .

I know that I have a choice. I can try to bluff it out, look as puzzled as everyone else and wait for this awkward moment to pass, or I can come clean, come out, meet Jesus, look him in the eye and say, 'Thank you.' He's not moving, in spite of his friends trying to get him to walk on, with Jairus looking more and more anxious. Jesus must think that this is important. Perhaps it is. Perhaps I have to complete the circle and face my past and my future full on. Perhaps there's more at stake here than simply fixing the mess of my menstrual cycle.

All right. Here I go.

I step forward, head up, eyes fixed on Jesus. He knows. His face is one big, warm smile. When I get close, I find that somehow I'm on the ground and I'm starting to pour out my story. I can't believe that he just kneels down right alongside me in the dust. It would be embarrassing if it wasn't so generous. He takes my hand. No one has done that willingly for years. Touch!

And he says something beautiful: 'Daughter of God, you are loved, and your faith is lovely to see. It's made you well; do you know that? So now you can go in peace. You're healed. You're safe in God's hands.' It was something like that anyway. I just know that I'm overwhelmed a second time. I feel completely assured of God's love for me and that I'm safe. Is this what they mean by salvation?

It's all too much to take in. With a last conspiratorial smile, he gets up and walks on with an agitated Jairus beside him. He leaves behind one amazed and grateful woman.

I'm so glad he asked who touched him.

• • •

Do we reach out to touch Jesus?

There's a pilgrimage centre on the western shore of the Sea of Galilee. It was built by the Catholic Church on the site of the excavated fishing village of Magdala, where Mary Magdalene came from. Among the chapels in the beautiful main building is the Encounter Chapel and, on the wall behind the altar, there is a large mural of the woman who had been suffering from bleeding reaching out to touch the hem of Jesus' robe. All you see is a ground-level view of her hand, about to make contact with Jesus' robe. The effect is electric. A second later, her life changed.

'Who touched me?'

The woman's healing comes in two stages. The first illustrates how touch has the power to heal, while the second shows how important it is to move beyond shame if we're to receive full restoration and freedom.

The woman stretched out her hand to touch any part of Jesus' clothing that she could. She was responding to the popular, almost magical, belief that simply touching a healer could have the desired effect. There was no lack of such healers in Jesus' day, nor were they viewed as charlatans. We have no idea how Jesus' healing power worked, but that he did heal many people during his ministry is attested to by all contemporary witnesses. The importance of touch in those healings is very often central to them. Jesus touched blind eyes, deaf ears, despised lepers and many, many more.

Our own experience also points to the importance of touch. A baby needs to be touched and held, needs to feel the reassuring warmth of its mother's skin. The gentle touch of the loved one is sweet ecstasy to couples. When somebody has been bereaved, one of the most acute deprivations is that of touch. When the COVID-19 pandemic was at its height, one of the most painful losses was that of human touch, particularly in hospitals and care homes. It was often said at the time that a computer couldn't give you a hug. Humans are made for presence, touch and embrace.

Theologian David Ford once visited a community where people with and without learning disabilities live and work together, and he wrote:

Touching is basic. It flows through the day – dressing, eating, carrying, haircare, bathing, playing, and just literally keeping in touch. Above all what struck me was its gentleness. The violence of our times is horrendous – physical violence, verbal violence, economic violence, institutional violence, spiritual violence. It is intensified by being vividly presented in the media, so that violence dominates imaginations as well as behaviour. Yet here in this place was a practice of touching, of handling people, which seemed like a prophetic sign of an alternative. It had enabled gentleness to be at the heart of this community.[11]

The woman with the debilitating bleeding believed that just to touch Jesus, even to touch only his clothes, would be enough, and it was. There's power in the simplicity of touch. Moreover, we continue to draw on this imagery in our worship, prayer, hymns and songs. We pray for the touch of Christ for those who are ill. We open ourselves to the touch of God in our personal prayers. A much loved hymn contains this verse:

> The healing of his seamless dress
> Is by our beds of pain;
> We touch him in life's throng and press,
> And we are whole again.[12]

Jesus himself honoured the potency and importance of touch when he turned round in the crowd and asked, 'Who touched me?' The disciples' reply was ironic. When people were crowding in from every direction, wasn't it a bit ridiculous to ask who had touched him? Jesus, though, knew that something significant had happened. He was 'immediately aware that power had gone forth from him' (v. 30), so he asked, 'Who touched me?'

When we pray, we are reaching out to touch Jesus.

That leads us to the second part of the woman's healing. Jesus wasn't prepared to leave her with the job half done. He wanted more for her than simply the relief from her physical symptoms that she was longing for. He wanted her to receive the whole gift that awaited her. That's why he asked, 'Who touched me?' When someone has been cured by the power that inevitably flows from one who is so deeply in tune with his Father, then that cure needs to be transformed into full healing, and full healing involves relationship. The woman needed to come out from behind the wall of shame where she'd been hiding and step into the full light of her divine restoration – a restoration that was social, spiritual and psychological as well as physical. That was salvation.

That's a step many people find incredibly hard to take. The alcoholic who refuses to acknowledge his situation and the mayhem it's causing, and seek help; the young mother whose brightness covers a brittle self-image that's cracking under the overwhelming demands of motherhood; the middle-aged couple who go through the motions of marriage without being able to admit that it's falling apart; the teenage girl who despairs of her body image and thinks self-harming will deflect her demons. Society is littered with hidden shame.

It takes huge courage to come out of the crowd and admit your need. In a fragmented and individualistic society, we are convinced that self-reliance is a necessary virtue. We must 'learn to stand on our own two feet', people say, because, 'the weak go to the wall' and 'God helps those who help themselves'. We admire self-confidence and train people in assertiveness. We live in a 'me-first' culture where the Big Me mustn't show weakness, whatever vulnerabilities lie underneath.

The resulting havoc is a major social crisis. It presents huge problems for psychiatrists, counsellors, therapists, schools, families and helping agencies of all sorts. As a society, we need to learn again that to admit need is not weakness but the beginning of resilience and recovery. When I collapsed with stress and nervous exhaustion after a wonderful but hugely demanding youth weekend for 600 young people in Wells many years ago, the first move towards healing was to stop pretending, somewhat arrogantly, that I could do anything, endure anything and achieve anything if I just had enough time. I needed to go and find that God-given doctor who could see what was going on and give me an understanding of stress, a book of ancient Scripture and firm instructions to sleep on demand. I needed to face my vulnerabilities and feelings of failure.

'Who touched me?' We need to listen to the question that Jesus asks and come out from behind our defences to find understanding, help and freedom. That is 'salvation' by any other name.

One final point for all of us who lead busy Christian lives. When this poor woman stopped Jesus in his tracks, he was already on important business. He was on his way to Jairus's house, where the Jewish leader's beloved little daughter was on the point of death. Yet Jesus was prepared to take the time to handle this interruption, on which a woman's health and happiness depended. Church life today is often driven by strategies, objectives, priorities and agendas, but one of the most important lessons we can learn as Christians is that God often meets us most of all in the interruptions. The much loved spiritual guide Henri Nouwen wrote:

> My whole life I have been complaining that my work was constantly interrupted, until I discovered that my interruptions *were* my work.[13]

May we always have time to stop and ask, like Jesus, 'Who touched me?' so that we can help others with their needs. May we also never tire of reaching out to touch Jesus so that we can be healed.

To ponder

- I wonder how the woman's life in the village went on after she was healed?
- When has your experience of touch been most helpful?
- Have you ever dared to come out from behind your shame or embarrassment about something? What was the effect of that on you and on others?
- How do you cope with interruptions?

Prayer

A is for intercession; B is more contemplative.

A Give thanks for those who held you and gave you love as a child, and for those who do so now. Pray for people you either know or suspect didn't receive much love as a child, and for people who seem deprived of tangible expressions of love now.

B In your imagination, go to a place where you feel secure, happy and at peace – perhaps a place from childhood or holidays. Stay there for a while, be comfortable and rest in the experience. Don't follow your thoughts too much; just notice them and let them float away. Relax in your chosen place and enjoy God's peace.

7

'What did you go out into the wilderness to look at?'
Luke 7.24 (18–35)

I hope we haven't been disloyal. I like to think that we've done what John himself suggested in moving on from him to Jesus. It's true that my wife Miriam and I were captivated with John when he was baptizing hundreds of us down at the Jordan. He was such a compelling figure, a no-nonsense, say-it-like-it-is preacher – a real breath of fresh air in the stale atmosphere of our faltering national hopes. We longed for genuine prophetic voices.

Miriam heard of him first, while she was fetching water one morning. (The well is the best place in the village for information and gossip.) She picked up that this wild character was attracting crowds from far and wide, even from Jerusalem. People weren't put off, even though he was always preaching about the need for us to repent because we were an ungodly lot in an ungodly nation. He wasn't tailoring his message to his listeners or trying to win any popularity contest. 'Brood of vipers' was one phrase we heard him use. I still can't work out why we liked being told off so much. Perhaps we genuinely recognized the truth about ourselves for once.

Anyway, we went and found him in the desert, down by the Jordan, and we got baptized, Miriam and I, and it was an amazing experience. A long queue snaked down to the water. I felt quite nervous as we got closer and closer. John was shouting and baptizing, shouting and baptizing, but people came up out of the water shining. It was the same with us. This grizzled figure seized hold of me, dragged me underwater without apology and held me down there until I was desperate to get out and breathe again. When I did, it felt as if I was made new – the life-giving wonder of that first breath, the glorious colours, the light streaming from the water. I can feel it now.

That made it all the more tragic when we heard John had been arrested and thrown into one of Herod's prisons down south.

We'd heard him say, a number of times, though, that he was only like a road sweeper before a great procession. He was a herald preparing us for the hero. He wasn't even worthy, he said, of untying the straps on the hero's sandals. 'I've baptized you with water,' he said, 'but this holy one will give you something much greater, something that will turn your lives inside out.'

So here we are, listening to Jesus.

To Miriam and me it's been fascinating seeing how different they are, John and Jesus, and yet how connected. Jesus can be fierce, too – we've seen him send Pharisees away with their tails between their legs – but there's a calm centre to him somehow, an authority, a confidence. It's not arrogance – he loves playing with children, damming streams with them, seeing who can get the most bounces from a skimming stone. No, not arrogance, more a centredness, a deep inner stillness. He seems completely at home with himself and completely at peace with God.

Meantime, there's poor John, languishing in a cell at the mercy of Herod and his vixen wife – the one who was married to Philip before Herod stole her, which John doesn't let her forget.

Jesus is sitting on a felled tree trunk lying near the shoreline. We're gathered round, close up so that we can hear him best, sitting on grass and rocks, wherever we can. What's happening now is really interesting to Miriam and me because two young men we recognize from our time with John have come to see Jesus with a message from John himself.

We listen. John's message is something like, 'Are you the one we've been waiting for or should we wait for someone else?' I wonder how it must feel to John, hearing what Jesus is doing, but hearing it second hand. Is he puzzled because Jesus isn't being as confrontational as he wants or is he just wanting to hear it direct from Jesus' mouth – 'Yes, I'm the one.' Who knows? A bit of both probably.

Anyway, Jesus looks at the two young guys for a moment, weighing them up. 'You've been with us for a bit, haven't you?' he asks. They nod. 'So you've seen what we've been doing. People have been healed, regained their sight, the lame are walking again, lepers are made clean, the deaf are hearing – praise God! You've seen it? So tell John. Be witnesses. Then let him make up his mind.' He smiles at them. They smile back, remembering what they've seen. Then they get up and set off on their long journey back to John.

Jesus watches them go, also remembering, lost in thought for a while.

Dear John. What will he make of this? Jesus hasn't said in so many words, 'I'm the one, the Messiah; you got it right.' If he is the one John meant, he's being clever in not claiming too much when rumour has it that Herod is after his life as well. Whatever the case, as John and Jesus, our two heroes, connect in this strange way by the lakeside, I find myself really hoping that John will be satisfied. Really hoping.

Then Jesus turns to us, as if suddenly remembering we're here, and puts us all right on the spot.

'So what did you go out into the wilderness to see?'

Yes, why did Miriam and I go into the desert so willingly? What did we want to see? It's hard to pin down. Jesus suggests that maybe we went to see a reed blowing in the wind. Strange picture, but Herod has reeds on his coins – perhaps Jesus is asking if we expected to find another king. Did we go out to see someone dressed in soft robes and feeding on figs, yogurts and expensive fruits? Well, we certainly didn't get that! What was it then? Were we looking for a prophet?

Ah, yes, a prophet. I think that was it for the two of us. Here was a battering ram of a figure, like the old prophets we've heard about but never seen – until now.

'What did you go out into the wilderness to look at?'

'You know what?' says Jesus. 'John is even more than a prophet. In the old order of things there's been no one greater. In the new order of things, though – the kingdom – he wouldn't actually count as anything special.'

Miriam gasps beside me. I can hear her thinking, 'How can he put John down like that?' but as Jesus goes on, I think I might be getting it. He's saying something even more radical than we've dared to imagine concerning this 'kingdom of God' that he keeps talking about. John has been wonderful; he's done everything that could have been asked of a forerunner. But the coming kingdom is blazingly different. If I remember my Malachi right (scraping the memory here) the prophet would clear the way for the Master to come to the Temple and clean it up. Unholiness would be swept away; God's justice and mercy would fill not only the Temple but also all Israel. Yet, 'Who can endure the day of his coming, and who can stand when he appears?'

I remember those words used to send a shiver down my spine. This new order of things would be so different, those who belonged to the old order – even John – would be left in the shadows. The new light would be just too dazzling.

I can't wait! At least, I don't think I can . . .

• • •

'What did you go out into the wilderness to see?'

It's actually more likely that we haven't gone into the wilderness in the first place. The wilderness is the place where our faith is tested to see what it's really made of. It's where we go if we're serious about wanting to grow, but it's not for the faint-hearted. Most of us are happier in the safety of Sunday morning church.

I once trekked for a week across part of the Sinai desert. A week without a road or a telegraph pole; a week where the only light was from the sun, the stars and a torch; a week sleeping outside on the desert floor without tent or pillow; a week with a few friends and with God. What I remember is the extremes of temperature, the sudden wind at dusk, the grumpiness of the camels, the friendliness of the Bedouin and the luxury of silence.

We spent the first two hours of every day walking in silence. We let the desert speak. We had stripped away most of our conventional supports and comforts; all that remained was to expose ourselves to the complexities and ambiguities of our own lives, suddenly alone in the presence of God. For myself, it was a time of emptiness and fullness, awareness and mystery, anxiety and joy. In a sense, we were making a break for freedom. Not running away from ourselves but running *towards* our true selves, freed for a while from our compulsions, our anxious comparisons, our status seeking, our obsession with 'stuff' and our endless chatter.

In the desert we come face to face with ourselves. We can't simply push the pedal to the floor, try harder, pray more and immerse ourselves in 'Five Ways to Get Closer to God'. No wonder we resist going into the wilderness without at least wi-fi, headphones and a large supply of chocolate.

From the third century onwards, as the Roman Empire embraced Christianity and compromised its countercultural message, more and more Christians went into the desert. They did so not to escape from the complexities of life but to engage with the life of the world from a completely different angle. There they faced their own demons and the demonic forces that stalk the world of wealth and power. They were going to the front line in the battle for the soul of the world. They were serious about their faith and the needs of humanity.

The desert has been the location of many of the most critical spiritual encounters in the story of our faith. Israel went through 40 years of desert wanderings; Elijah heard that 'still, small voice' in the mountains; Jesus had a fierce battle with temptation in the desert; Paul spent three years sorting out his theology in the deserts of Arabia; the 'desert fathers' have inspired the faithful for 1,700 years. So often, the wilderness has been the context for deep encounters with God. It's the same today. In the frenetic marketplace of life, we all have several numbers and are known by algorithms; in the desert we have a name and are known by God.

The desert is a spiritual and psychological place as well as a geographical one. There are deserts in cities, deserts in ordinary life, deserts within each one of us. We just have to want to go there. But why take the risk? What would we go out into the wilderness to see?

It's been the consistent teaching of the Church that the spiritual life is more about subtraction than addition. Our consumer-driven, competitive culture wants us to achieve, succeed and amass more and more things. Authentic spirituality, shaped by the model of Jesus, is about letting go, stripping away and simplifying. It's as clear as it is daunting.

It's no wonder that we resist going into the desert, but this is a significant moment of choice in our life with God. This is where 'Yes' and 'No' collide, where we have to decide how serious we are about moving further along this path of faith. What do we want to go out into the wilderness to see? Do we want to go at all?

Setting off starts, I believe, with a decision to opt for simplicity, stillness and silence, for stories and sacraments, for mystery and paradox, for travelling lightly through the world. Even such a capacious mind as that of Albert Einstein could believe, 'A table, a chair, a bowl of fruit and a violin – what else does a man [sic] need to be happy?'

It's interesting that so many people today are drawn to the simplicity of running, cycling and fishing (our number one pastime). There's a hunger to declutter, to take up mindfulness, yoga or t'ai chi. There's a huge desire to simplify through these secular forms of what spirituality means by 'the desert', the place of subtraction.

In a 'decluttered' spiritual space, Christians can begin to take risks and try other ways to meet with God. For some people this might involve reading Scripture in a different way, taking it slowly, noticing a phrase that stands out, chewing it to get all the goodness out of it, then praying about what they've received. That's called *lectio divina* or holy reading. For other people, taking a 'desert risk' might involve entering gospel stories with the senses, being present in the story and watching, hearing, touching what's going on, then finally talking with Jesus about it all. That's called 'Ignatian meditation'.

Other people might want to explore a spirituality more engaged with the natural world or one with music as the dominant gift.

The arts in general offer ways for many people to come closer to the experience of transcendence. We might want to look into Orthodox spirituality, especially the use of icons and the continuous saying of the Jesus Prayer ('Lord Jesus Christ, Son of God, have mercy on me, a sinner'). Some of us will want to go on pilgrimage to the Holy Land, Rome, Santiago, Assisi, Lindisfarne, Iona or even our local cathedral – the choice is huge. Going on retreat for the first time can be quite scary, but the silence can soon become an essential part of life. Finding a spiritual director can cause us alarm because we imagine that the poverty of our spiritual cupboard will finally be exposed, but the experience is almost always enriching.

All these, and scores more, are examples of taking the risk of going out into the desert to find 'something more' in our relationship with God. Perhaps the core of the desert experience, however, is that gift of silence, which we discover when we stop hiding behind the wall of words we so often put between ourselves and God and expose ourselves to the pure, unbounded love of God. Contemplative prayer enables us to experience prayer as a kind of pure sunbathing – simply going out and lying in the sun, not trying to turn up the heat but content to surrender to the sunlight, to let the sun be the sun, to let God be God.

A young journalist once interviewed Mother Teresa and asked about how she prayed. 'What words do you use when you pray to God?' she asked. Mother Teresa replied, 'I don't speak much to God; I just listen to him.' Slightly nonplussed, the journalist asked, 'What does God say?' 'Oh, he listens too,' said Mother Teresa. In contemplative prayer, we no longer analyse, make judgements or try to control anything. We let things be as they really are. We let God be the reference point rather than ourselves and simply be, alongside him.

'What did you go out into the wilderness to see?' It's a great question. Perhaps the answer is, 'I don't know.'

Or maybe the answer is, 'Yes.'

'What did you go out into the wilderness to look at?'

To ponder

- I wonder what so many people were looking for when they went out into the wilderness to meet John?
- I wonder how the disciples reacted when they heard that call to 'lose their lives' in order to save them?
- How do you hear that call – as threat, promise, fanciful, impossible or what?
- How do you react to that image of the desert and the call to explore quieter, riskier forms of spirituality?

Prayer

A is for intercession; B is more contemplative.

A Pray for anyone you know who seems to be lost in a wilderness of some sort. Pray about anything you might do to help.

B Explore your own desert. Try setting aside 10 to 15 minutes a day for silence. Settle down, be relaxed but alert and simply give the time to God, using a biblical word or phrase to 're-centre' when your mind inevitably wanders off.

8

'Do you also wish to go away?'
John 6.67 (52–71)

I'm one of the quieter followers, I suppose. Mostly I listen and keep my counsel. I won't give you my name, if you don't mind. I'm naturally a bit cautious.

I'm fascinated by Jesus, of course. I've never heard anyone like him. I feel really privileged that he asked me to join him and the others, but it doesn't mean I understand everything that's going on. I'm still trying to work it out.

We've had an amazing couple of days. It started on the other side of the lake when we had a huge crowd to hear Jesus' teaching, but no idea how to feed them. The trouble was, we hadn't expected it to go on so long, but they just wouldn't let Jesus go and it got late and there was no food. At least, I *thought* there was no food, then a bit later, it seemed that there was actually enough food for everyone, and then some. I can't explain it.

Anyway, the day was practically over by then. The crowd started to go home. We climbed into one of the boats – without Jesus. He was still chatting with some of the more eager members of the crowd; there are always some who can't drag themselves away. It was dark out in the middle of the lake and it was getting rough as well. What happened out there – well, I don't think I trust myself to talk about it yet. It's just too difficult to sort out in my head. Can we leave it there for the moment?

Anyway, today's another day.

There's a big discussion going on down at the lake shore with some of those who were around yesterday, mostly our regulars. There are quite a few of us now, travelling around with Jesus or turning up when he's teaching. There's a core of us who Jesus picked out early on, and there are some very generous women who support us, who often come along with us too. Then there are lots of other people who seem to belong to us in different ways, new ones joining us as they get hooked by Jesus' teaching, others having to drop out to get home or back to work.

So here we are in this big discussion. Today, there must be 30 or 40 of us, but I can tell that some in the group are getting a bit restless. I have a particular friend called Jacob. He's sitting with me on a rock, looking out over the lake, but he seems uneasy; he doesn't usually fidget so much. Jesus is talking about bread, but he's moved on from the bread we found for that crowd yesterday. He's talking about *him* somehow *being* the bread we need – God's bread or bread from heaven or the bread of life, something like that.

That is what's making Jacob so obviously uncomfortable. I think it's all getting a bit too intense for him. He was happier when Jesus spent most of his time around Capernaum and we had that great teaching about the kingdom of God, and those amazing healings. It was all so exciting. But now I can sense that it's going a bit too far for Jacob and some of the others. For them, Jesus is going over the top, claiming too much. They just want to cool it all down and go back to the simpler stuff. You can almost hear them thinking, 'Couldn't we go back and start again?'

Jacob turns to speak to another lad sitting alongside him. I'm not sure of his name. Benny, I think. They talk to each other quietly, lots of nodding between them. Finally, Jacob and Benny get up. Jacob says to me, 'Sorry, mate. I'll see you.' He raises a hand of farewell to Jesus – reluctantly, it seems, but with a kind of finality. Jesus raises a hand too, in a way that's both sad and kind. I can see others slipping away as well. In fact, it's a steady stream, some of my friends included. They surprise me. I can tell that most of them are embarrassed.

Silence hangs over the lake shore, except for the soothing sound of the waves lapping gently on the beach. I look out over the lake, reassured by the familiar shape of the hills on the far side. Some things don't change.

Those of us who are left move in closer around Jesus. He looks at each one of us wistfully. 'Do you also want to go away?' he asks. He's giving us the choice, to go back or to go on. It's an important question, somehow both an offer and an invitation. Different kinds of freedom.

There's a pause. The distant sound of a shepherd. Children playing happily nearby. Wind gently rustling the trees.

As I say, I'm not a leader in this group. I'm not noisy. Peter is, of course – and we love him – so it's not surprising that he's the one who speaks up. We can tell that he wants to rally us, restore our confidence, as well as to reassure Jesus. 'Are we going away too? No way,' he says. 'Who else would we go to? You've got everything we need. We're sure now that you're the One, God's chosen One. We're staying.'

Peter's got it right, of course. He speaks for us all. I haven't got it all sorted in my mind, though. Half the time I'm really confused by what's going on around me, what I see and hear, but I'm committed. Jesus has asked me to go with him. I can't imagine why, but he's cleverer than me, so I must fit in somehow. Maybe I'll be able to do something useful when the time comes.

Jesus smiles at us. Grateful. He turns and leads the way back along the lake shore. There are 12 of us.

I realize that I'm smiling.

• • •

'Do you also want to go away?'

Here's another way of putting it: have you ever sat in church and wondered if there was something else you'd rather be doing with your Sunday morning? Not that services have to be exciting all the time, but many people have felt the sad drift of a church that's gone stale. A Christian couple took their offspring to their church one Christmas and one of them said afterwards, 'That's the last time I'll ever take anyone there. There was no attempt to enliven the story, no interest in engaging our attention. The liturgy was lifeless and the language flat. I was embarrassed that I'd asked anyone along.'

'Do you also want to go away?' Many people have. They've left the Church for any number of reasons – boredom with its worship, irritation with its leaders, saddened by its small agendas, disillusioned by its lack of depth, hurt by its disciplines and so on. We rightly have high expectations of the Church as a holy community, called to live differently, so we feel all the more let down when it turns out to be as flawed as any other human institution. A comedian once quipped, 'I've come to view Jesus the way I view Elvis. I love the guy, but the fan club really freaks me out.'

Other people leave because they've been scared by the scale of the gospel challenge, as was the case with some of those early followers of Jesus. They come to realize that the gospel involves a thorough overhaul of our priorities, motives, life choices . . . indeed, our whole world-view. In particular, it involves a fierce allegiance to Jesus, a man unlike any other. They decide it is too much and slip away. As Mark Twain is reputed to have said, 'It's not the parts of the gospel that I don't understand which cause me difficulty – it's the demand of that which I do understand.'

Have you ever wanted to go away?

It might be helpful to widen our thinking here because there are many different ways in which people can legitimately belong to God and the Church, so the idea of 'going away' is a bit complex. Bishop David Walker, in his book *God's Belongers*, suggests four different modes of belonging – by means of:

- **church activities** including worship, home groups, pastoral care, social action;
- **relationships** including home visits, getting the parish magazine, online contact;
- **events** including baptisms, weddings, funerals and key festivals in the Christian calendar;
- **places** especially church buildings, as visible symbols of 'something more' in a transient and sometimes trivial society.[14]

All these are legitimate ways of belonging and we miss a trick if we reduce our canvas to include only those who come to church.

It may well be the case that there are, in fact, many people in our churches who are sitting on the edge of things, not quite sure they're in the right place, but unwilling to turn away completely. I always want to ask such 'finger-nail' believers to resist being part of the First Battalion Innocent Bystanders or the rag-tag army of those who wanted to change the world but couldn't get a babysitter. My message, always, is to stay in the Church and make things better! If you take a log out of the fire it will glow for a while but eventually it will go out. Our faith, too, may go out when it loses contact with the place where the spiritual fire is visibly burning. To use a different image, the Church is like Noah's ark: that old boat must have smelt pretty bad inside, but if you jumped out, you'd drown.

Of course, the Church fails. So does every other human organization or system – politics, education, health care, law, the City. The human body fails too – indeed, it's never completely healthy. Generally it functions pretty well, but we're never completely whole, some part of it always niggles. So it is with the Church. If we leave this body of believers, we'll miss the glorious messy muddle that is God's Church – the acts of love and courage, of sanity and saintliness, that happen there. Of course, the Church is both magnificent and bonkers. So are we. We are the rusty containers into which the clear, pure water of the gospel has been poured, and the water we pour out, sadly, is mingled with the rust.

There are two mistakes that we can make in relation to the Church. One is to take it too seriously; the other is not to take it seriously enough. When we take the Church too seriously, we make it the indispensable ark of salvation, but God is our Saviour, not the Church. The Church tells the story of God, as Jesus did, opening it out before his listeners. If we focus on the Church as an organization, though, we risk becoming irrelevant; we become managers and salespeople of 'the right system' rather than storytellers for Jesus. In the words of Brian McLaren:

[Jesus] never announced to his disciples: 'Hey folks, we're going to start a new, centralized, institutional religion and name it after me.' Instead, he played the role of a nonviolent leader and launched his movement with the classic words of movement, 'Follow me'. . .[15]

The Church is a body of people who have been captivated by the life and teaching of Jesus and are now seeking to follow him into a new way of living, a new world.

One of the prime features of an institution is its buildings, but God mustn't be held captive by churches. In the novel *The Color Purple* by Alice Walker, Shug Avery, one of the unlikely heroes of the story, is talking to Celie. She says:

'Celie, tell the truth, have you ever found God in church? I never did. I just found a bunch of folks hoping for him to show. Any God I ever felt in church I brought in with me. And I think all the other folks did too. They come to church to *share* God, not to *find* God.'[16]

When we do come together, though, God is present, he 'shows'. At its best, the Church is a place where everyone is welcome, no one is perfect and nothing is impossible – because God shows up.

'Do you also want to go away?' Please don't. It's God who matters. Leaving the Church would be sad, but leaving God – or leaving Jesus, as some of those followers did that day – would be even more serious.

Of course, that is precisely the journey many people in our culture have been on – taking leave of God. The stakes are much higher here, but some have found that God, or the idea of God, has disappointed them just as much as the Church. One reason for this has been intellectual. For example, some have failed to distinguish between science – which Christians should celebrate – and *scientism,* which is the view that only science has got anything to say about the nature of human life in the universe. The tragedy of this latter view is that it drastically limits the worlds of evidence available to us – the insights of philosophers, artists, theologians, poets, historians . . .

A further reason people give for 'going away' from God is disappointment with what God does and doesn't do in a world beset with problems. God doesn't intervene arbitrarily to sort out the multitude of issues we face as a society or as individuals. Indeed, he seems to remain stubbornly silent and elusive just when we want him most. Why? Is it asking too much? In other words, God disappoints us because he's not what we want God to be.

The trouble is, God can't help being God. God is the way God is, and he takes responsibility for that, and for the world and its disappointments. God made the world and its inhabitants to enjoy a mature and radical freedom – obviously, because that's the nature of Love. That freedom includes not being forced to believe in God by sheer weight of evidence and the volume of his voice. God walks quietly through the world. He whispers, although it's a whisper that has captivated humanity. Moreover, God took responsibility for 'the way the world is' with such seriousness that he died for it. God (in Christ) died for love of the world and its freedom.

> See from his head, his hands, his feet
> Sorrow and love flow mingled down.
> Did e'er such love and sorrow meet
> Or thorns compose so rich a crown?[17]

'Do you also want to go away?' I hope not. I wouldn't dare leave a love as rich and profound as that.

To ponder

- I wonder how the followers who left Jesus felt afterwards?
- Have you ever felt like leaving the Church? How did you handle that?
- Why do you go to church – really?

Prayer

A is for intercession; B is more contemplative.

A Give thanks for those who have stayed with you through thick and thin in your life. Pray for any you know who have been left by a partner, children, friends.
B Practise the presence of God now and during the day. This means pausing and simply remembering the unfailing presence of God. Look in God's direction for a moment and acknowledge the relationship, even at the heart of a busy day. It's like exchanging a smile with God, then getting on with life.

9

'But who do you say that I am?'
Mark 8.29 (27–38)

We were in high spirits as we set off. It had been a hectic few
months around the lake and Jesus was taking us away for a break.
He does that every so often. Once, he took us up to the sea for the
best part of a week – somewhere near Tyre, I seem to remember.

Actually, now I think about it, there was quite a disturbing
incident while we were there. A young woman found us and had
a go at Jesus for not being prepared to help her with her sick
daughter. They had a bantering kind of conversation but, essentially, she got Jesus to back down, if you can believe that. He was
saying that he'd come to help his own people, us Jews, and she was
saying, 'That's all very well, but we Gentiles need help as well,' and
Jesus conceded that she was right – and he healed her daughter.

I was a little troubled by this, I admit. What we Jews need most
of all is to get our country back from those arrogant Romans. We
have to stay focused on that. I had a word with Jesus afterwards,
to make the point that this was no time to go soft. He just smiled
and said that there was room for all in the kingdom of God.
Personally, I think he allowed himself to be charmed by that
feisty young woman.

Anyway, back to our recent retreat up on the slopes of Mount
Hermon. We were way up the Jordan Valley, near a place called
Caesarea Philippi, named after both the emperor himself and
Philip, the ruler round here. Too much Roman influence for my
liking, but it got us away from the crowds following us round the
lake. We wanted some rest, and I think Jesus wanted to get some
distance from all that's been happening recently, clear his head

a bit. He chose the right place. From up there, on a clear day, you can see right down the Jordan Valley to Galilee, and even beyond, towards Jerusalem. It's a glorious sight. We could take in the view of the whole region where Jesus had been stirring things up.

So this is what happened. We'd had a wonderful, relaxed day. We got up when we liked. We ate, we played games, we joked, we swam in the mountain pools, we made fun of Matthew when he seemed determined to find out how much tax they charged around there. We had a great time. Then, as the afternoon heat was dying down and the sun was painting everything a rich gold, Jesus called us together. He had some questions that he wanted to ask, he said.

We sat in a circle, on rocks and tree trunks, whatever was available, and I looked around at my young friends. I'm a bit older than them – they make me pay for it sometimes! They were eager, fresh-faced, impressionable, and utterly devoted to Jesus. That was obvious. He could have told them to walk on water and they'd have had a go.

He came straight at us with the first question. 'Who do people say that I am?' he asked. Well, that was easy enough. 'John the Baptist,' said Andrew. 'Elijah,' said Thaddaeus. (I was glad he spoke up. He usually keeps pretty quiet.) 'One of the prophets,' said someone else. We used to hear what people were saying while we were organizing the crowds, getting them to bunch up and so on. Sometimes they asked us what we thought of Jesus. 'You just listen,' I used to say.

Jesus smiled a bit ruefully, nodding as he received our answers, but then he swung back with the really big question. He looked each of us straight in the eye as he went round the circle and said, 'And you, who do you say that I am?'

Silence. Birds singing innocently. A goat stirring nearby. He waited.

Who was going to speak first? What did we really think, I wondered, this group of friends who had been with him all this time, watched him, listened to him, seen the amazing things that he did? What were we prepared to say? I was still working on it. Still am, in fact. I knew who I *wanted* him to be. We'd been waiting for him long enough, but, as a people, we'd been disappointed so often.

Anyway, there was no more time for pondering. Peter, as ever, came up with the goods. 'You're the Messiah,' he said, looking straight at Jesus, daring him to disagree.

Well, he didn't, but he did say what he often says. 'Just keep quiet on that please. It's important.'

Why is it important? It gets to me, but I think it's like this. He wants to put some distance between what *we* think the Messiah should be like and who he actually sees himself as being, which is rather different. That's what I've concluded and I'm not very comfortable with it. We all know that the Messiah will be the heir of David, the true King of Israel – not one of these pale copies we've had to put up with for so many years.

He'll clear out the invaders, sort out the Temple and start a proper reign of justice and, hopefully, real peace. As I see it, if the Messiah isn't going to do that, what's he for?

But here was Jesus saying what I feared, 'Don't tell anyone', as if he was embarrassed! Then he started telling us some completely wild stuff about being rejected wholesale by the Temple authorities (fair enough), suffering (why?), then having to die (that was crazy) and rise again (what *was* going on here?).

I wasn't surprised that Peter went over to Jesus, took him by the elbow and tried to steer him away for a quiet word – except that we could hear that 'quiet word'. Peter argued with Jesus, something along the lines of 'Come on, Jesus, the Messiah can't get killed, that's just daft.' And we heard Jesus' answer, because he intended us to: 'Clear off, you Satan.'

Yes, he really did say that.

I have to say, that felt inexcusable. Peter was just being kind and trying to put Jesus straight, but Jesus was really serious. Peter had obviously touched a sore spot, maybe a memory of dealing with Satan on some other occasion. Jesus then proceeded to tell us in no uncertain terms that if we wanted to be his followers, we had to put ourselves aside, carry our own cross (horrible image), then follow this hard, hard way.

We were stunned. The evening light was warm. We sat silently. Everything was crystal clear. Too clear.

Some Messiah this, I thought. Have we got it all wrong? Have we got time to sort it out?

My name is Judas, by the way. Judas Iscariot.

• • •

There are two important questions here: 'Who do people say that I am?' followed by 'Who do *you* say that I am?'. One of the few sermons I remember from my undergraduate days made the case that these were the two most important questions we would ever face. How clearly do you think you could answer the second one?

A related question is this: 'Who do you want him to be?' Because few people have been so 'put upon' as Jesus, constantly receiving our projections of the kind of Christ we want.

Do we want him to be a great human teacher? Yes, but more than that. Do we want him to be an all-time winner, one who zaps his enemies like the characters in video games do? No. What about a kind of spiritual Zen master, offering comfortable piety to ease our days? No, not that either. What we need is more like *uncomfortable* piety.

It's hard for us to let the startling figure of Jesus stand free of our expectations and projections. For every person with a particular picture of him, there's someone else with an alternative one. Oscar Wilde wrote, 'Christ's place is with the poets. His entire life is the most wonderful of poems.'[18] Then again, a poster I once saw said that he was 'a radical, non-violent teacher, a long-haired, brown-skinned, homeless, community organising Middle Eastern Jew'. Equally, Lord Hailsham wrote that he saw 'a laughing, joking Jesus, physically strong and active, fond of good company and a glass of wine, telling funny stories, giving nicknames to his friends, and holding his companions spellbound with his talk'.[19] Poet, community organizer, bon viveur – these are very different images.

Who do we say he is?

There's an undeniable strangeness about Jesus, but his extraordinary influence on Western culture – and beyond – cannot be doubted. Tom Holland's much acclaimed book *Dominion* makes the case powerfully. He concludes:

> To be a Christian is to believe that God became man, and suffered a death as terrible as any mortal has ever suffered. This is why the cross, that ancient symbol of torture, remains what it has always been: the fitting symbol of the Christian revolution. It is the audacity of it – the audacity of finding in a twisted and defeated corpse the glory of the creator of the universe – that serves to explain, more surely than anything else, the sheer strangeness of Christianity, and of the civilisation to which it gave birth. Today the power of this strangeness remains as alive as it has ever been . . . [We] all are heirs of the same revolution that has, at its molten heart, the image of a god dead on a cross.[20]

This enigma is made even more complex by the way that we've made a religious cult out of Jesus rather than simply following him out on to the streets. We've worshipped him more than we've followed him. Jesus didn't ask for our worship; he invited us to come on a journey into an alternative reality that he called the kingdom of God, where he took people from the edges of society and put them at the centre of things – lepers, prostitutes, children, tax collectors, the poor, the blind, outcasts.

A much respected Armenian priest was asked what he thought would happen if Jesus walked into Jerusalem today. He closed his eyes for a moment and then said quietly, 'Jesus would probably do now what he did then: take care of the poor, speak truth to power, and get himself killed.'

The key way in which Jesus lived was that he let go of ego and self-interest and gave himself to God and to others. His was a path of self-emptying. The Greek word preachers sometimes use for this is *kenosis*. He emptied himself in the incarnation. He emptied himself when helping others. He emptied himself most of all on the cross. And he told his hearers (us) that the only way to live was to die to ourselves and to give ourselves away, because only those who lose their lives will save them. We meet Jesus on the way down the ladder, not on the way up. Being a Christian isn't just about making a few adjustments to our normal, comfortable lives; it's about finding a new centre to our lives, and living outwards from that new centre.

'Who do you say that I am?'

Peter was getting there when he tried to answer Jesus' question at Caesarea Philippi. He saw the Messiah in Jesus, but he didn't yet see what that idea really meant.

Gradually, however, what he and his friends were coming to realize was that you couldn't separate the man from his father. It was a case of 'like Father, like Son'. His whole life was, purely and simply, an act of God. The real him – his centre, the bit that was most genuinely him – was focused and centred on God. That was the astonishing truth they were finding they had to come to terms with; that they couldn't speak of Jesus without in some way speaking of God. That was what pushed the needle into the red zone and led the religious leaders of the day to cry 'Blasphemy' and have him crucified.

What, then, do we find ourselves saying when we face that sharp question of who Jesus is for us? It depends on the unique way in which Jesus meets us and how he has already made some claim on our lives. For myself, I would say that I find in Jesus a *life-giver*, who came to give abundance to my daily experiences of living, to give Life to life. I find a *life-saver*, who defeated the powers of darkness both within me and around me, offering peace and hope to both me and the world. I find a *prophetic teacher* who excites, inspires and challenges me to a deeper concern for the world – and for the next person I meet. I find a *faithful friend* who somehow accompanies me through every experience of joy and sorrow. I find a *risen, ascended Lord* who encompasses this world and the next, and enables me to join the first Christians in their groundbreaking creed: 'Jesus is Lord.'

This is what I find in Jesus as he asks me, 'John, who do you say that I am?' There's something about him that won't let me go. Not that I want him to. This figure holds and captivates me, disturbs and challenges me. Who do I say that he is? He's my leading light, my moral compass, my morning star. I find him endlessly fascinating, mysterious, attractive, enigmatic and compelling. My Lord and my God.

In the last resort, I find myself wanting to echo St Anthony, who once called his two companions to him and said simply, 'Let your very breath be always Christ.'

I have a long way to go.

To ponder

- Why do you think Judas betrayed his friend?
- How do you react to the exchange that Jesus had with Peter, calling him Satan?
- How do you answer Jesus' question for yourself: 'Who do you say that I am?'
- How central is Jesus to your faith? Is it, instead, 'God' who's at the centre?

Prayer

A is for intercession; B is more contemplative.

A Pray for any ways in which you or your church are trying to share your faith in Jesus. Pray, too, for anyone you know who is considering the way of faith.

B Read slowly, and meditate on, a hymn or song that focuses on Jesus, such as 'At the name of Jesus', 'Jesus, name above all names', 'Lord Jesus Christ', 'My Jesus, my Saviour'.

10

'What do you want me to do for you?'
Mark 10.51 (46–52)

It's hot and I'm tired. Mind you, it's always hot in Jericho . . . and I'm usually tired as well. It's surprisingly tiring, sitting by the roadside day after day, hoping that people will give you something to help you get by. At the start of every day, I make my way here, where the road heads off to Jerusalem, and I sit under this tree, feeling pretty helpless, waiting for people to notice that I'm blind.

I wasn't always blind. When I was young I could see, though never well, but as I grew up and entered into my teenage years, I lost everything. It was frightening, finding that I could see less and less every week. I would wake up each day and test how much I could see around the room, desperately afraid that I might not be able to see as much as I did yesterday. Awful.

Anyway, this is what it led to. Darkness. So I sit and wait.

I suppose that you might call me a beggar. I'd prefer that you call me Bartimaeus, as I'm a person, the son of Timaeus, respected citizen of Jericho, but, undoubtedly, my job is begging. I know a lot of us have to do this, but that doesn't make it any easier. I have my dignity.

Jericho isn't a bad place to beg. A lot of people are passing through – pilgrims coming down the Jordan Valley from Galilee on their way to the steep, dangerous road to Jerusalem. Jericho is more on the map now, ever since Herod built his winter palace here. The thing is, Jerusalem gets cold in winter but because we're so much lower than the holy city, we never really get cold down here. That's both a blessing and a curse of course, as it does get so blisteringly hot. Some say we're the oldest city in the world, built round an oasis a few miles from the Jordan and that weird Dead Sea. I went swimming in it once – strangest water I've ever known; I couldn't have sunk even if I'd tried! Something to do with all the salt in the water.

The day is crawling by so slowly. A bit of money and a few pieces of fruit have been left on the edge of my cloak. My cloak is like a begging bowl I suppose, just a bit less embarrassing. As usual, a few lazy flies are annoying me. Also as usual, I've drunk nearly all my water.

Hold on a minute – something's changing. There seems to be a lot more people around me than usual. I don't know whether they're locals or pilgrims, but there's a definite buzz. Suddenly I'm alert. When I wake up like this, my friends say that I look like an animal sniffing the air. Not a nice image, but I think I know what they mean. I suppose when you can't see anything your other senses are sharpened and you develop instincts that everyone else has as well but doesn't need to use as much as I do.

Anyway, I know that there's somebody special approaching. Don't ask me how I know that; I just do. I know that it's not a flock of sheep, or a company of Roman soldiers, or a bunch of louts coming to make fun of us. I know that it's someone with a special aura. I know that this is important.

So I ask, 'Who is it?' I get the answer from somebody standing right beside me. 'Jesus, the teacher from Nazareth,' he says. I've heard of him and, before I know it, I'm shouting out. I'm shouting for him to notice me and help me. The words are torn out of me – I just know that I have to get hold of him. I'm shouting, 'Jesus, Son of David, take pity on me!'

How come I know to call him 'Son of David'? It's really odd. Perhaps I've heard others giving him that name, but it seems right anyway. Son of David. Yes, that's him.

I've no idea if he can hear me. It's like I'm shouting out in the dark, of course, but I know that I have to make a connection with him. In fact, I already feel that I have a connection; I just need him to feel it too.

People around me are trying to shut me up. 'Shut your mouth, Bartimaeus. You're embarrassing – stop shouting, will you?!' (That's one of the more polite things they're saying.) I guess I am pretty loud, but I just have to get through to him. 'Jesus, take pity! Take pity!'

And he does.

I know that he's stopped – I sense it – and he's calling for me. A thrill goes through me, physically. We're connected. He's felt it too. A couple of people standing nearby haul me to my feet. 'Cheer up!' they say. 'He's asking for you, you jammy beggar.' I don't care whether I'm a jammy beggar or not, the point is he actually wants to speak to me! I know that there are lots of other people around us, but it feels like it's just him and me.

I'm standing before him alone now. I lean in towards his voice. It might seem a bit odd, but the sounds I hear often feel like colours. His voice is mid-brown, smooth and reassuring, but, more importantly, what's he going to say? Better still, what's he going to do? I can sense that his attention is focused directly on me, though obviously I can't see it. If I say that it feels like he's looking right into me, do you understand what I mean? I'm not used to this kind of attention; most people look right past me.

Then he says something that takes me completely by surprise. 'What do you want me to do for you?'

For a moment, I'm lost for an answer. I thought it was so obvious, but then the question goes deep inside me and I realize that he's asking me an even bigger question than I thought. He's asking if I'm ready to give up everything I've known throughout my adult life. I've been a blind beggar in Jericho for as long as I can remember. I've not done a real day's work in my life; I've depended on others to look after my needs. Do I want to give all that up and be an independent working man with grown-up responsibilities, a proper citizen of Jericho like my father? That would be a huge change. Do I want it?

All that flashes through my mind. It is the right question to ask me, but I also know the answer straight away, and I'm prepared to say it in front of everyone.

'Teacher, let me see again.'

Yes, that *is* what I want. I'm prepared for the consequences. I really, really want to see.

But I sense that there's something more behind my answer, just as there was something more behind his question. I don't just want to see with my eyes; I want to see with my soul. I want to stay with this Jesus and look at life as he does. I want to sit at his feet and learn from him. I want to share his freedom.

Jesus gets that too. He says to me quietly and tenderly, 'Then, be free. Your faith has made you well.'

That's it. What my instinct was pointing to, what I hadn't quite identified, was faith. I trust him. I believe in him. I can be saved by him.

I feel a burning sensation in my eyes, but it isn't frightening. I blink. I see something. I blink a second, third, fourth time. I can see, I can really see! Tears, tears, more tears! Tears of joy. I sit on the ground in a daze. Seeing.

Eventually he takes me by the elbow, lifts me up and we walk off together, on the way to Jerusalem.

• • •

'What do you want me to do for you?' I wonder if you can imagine Jesus saying that to you. What would you say at this particular point in your life? Our answers now will be different from what they would have been ten years ago, and that's fine. What would we say now?

Bartimaeus wanted to see again, and that involved a huge step; it involved trust. Trust that Jesus really could help, and trust in where that might lead.

One of our biggest decisions in life is deciding who to trust. It's not just about friendships and a life partner; our whole social structure is built on trust. Take our financial system. The London Stock Exchange was set up between traders who knew and trusted one another. The motto they adopted was 'my word is my bond'. The world's banking system depends on this same trust and breaking it has serious consequences, as we saw in the 2008 financial crisis.

Trust is crucial in all walks of life. Trust in employers, in politicians, in doctors, trust in the water company when we turn on the tap, trust in teachers when we hand over our children to a nursery or school.

Trust is at the heart of faith, and the story of Bartimaeus and Jesus in Jericho is essentially one about trust. When Jesus asked him the seemingly innocent question 'What do you want me to do for you?' it was a question that operated at two levels. There was the obvious one about getting his sight back, and the deeper one about what he really wanted out of life. Did he want spiritual sight, did he want to be saved? Did he trust Jesus to give him what he wanted?

Bartimaeus is put forward in the Gospel as a model of faith. Earlier in Mark 10, Jesus asked James and John the same question: 'What do you want me to do for you?' They answered that they wanted power and prestige, to sit alongside Jesus in his kingdom, one on his right and one on his left. It's the world's answer. But Bartimaeus demonstrated a deeper faith than those uncomprehending disciples. He asked for sight, and the Gospel writers suggest that the sight he found was both physical and spiritual – sight and insight. He received the full gift of healing and salvation when he asked with faith.

He trusted.

A Bible translator working in West Africa was trying to find the right word for 'faith'. This particular African language didn't have an obvious equivalent, so he called in a local friend. He leaned back in his chair and asked his friend, 'What am I doing now?' The friend gave him the word for 'leaning'. He leant further back and asked, 'So what am I doing now?' 'Leaning further,' he was told. He then leant so far back that he was about to tip over and he asked, 'What now?' 'Leaning with all your weight,' said the friend in his local language. 'That's it,' said the translator, 'that's the word I want. Leaning with all your weight.'

That's precisely what many people in the West find so hard to do. We have many other supports to lean on – among them wealth, technology, good health care, stable government, solid legal systems and much more. We've laboriously built up an array of social structures to protect us. Yet many of these have been shown to be alarmingly vulnerable in the face of such events as the financial crash of 2008, the COVID-19 pandemic, the frightening forecasts of climate change, cyber and biological terrorism, the proliferation of nuclear weapons and the fragility of our political systems. Nations easily panic and revert to fight or flight responses. Trust in our structures is sometimes blind, sometimes only skin-deep. In what, in whom, can we trust?

Christians in the West doubtless share much of culture's anxious trust in the social structures that have been put together. Ultimately, however, Christian faith points to the great 'and yet' of the gospel. 'And yet' is one of my favourite phrases. There are many human securities we can enjoy, but they're fallible. All may fail, 'and yet' God will not let us down. We may be struck by Job-like disaster, 'and yet' God will not cease to hold us. The way ahead may look uncertain, 'and yet' we will not walk the way alone. Faith trusts in God at a deeper level than the circumstances at the time.

Bartimaeus didn't know where his life was going, but he knew that it was with Jesus, and he followed him 'on the way' – an obvious allusion to the early description of Christianity as 'the Way'. He took the first step. We don't know what happened to him when he got swallowed up in the events of Jerusalem in that last traumatic week and thereafter. We only know that he wanted a new start and he wanted to make it with Jesus. Millions of us have been on the same journey.

Faith isn't about guarantees; it's about risks. It doesn't depend on proofs, or need constant shoring up with emotional experiences. It isn't dependent on how often God jumps to our requests. Faith is a direction of travel. Faith is a journey to a place called home. But at each stage of that journey, we have to face the hard fact that faith isn't about safety. The best people, the nicest people, *our* people, experience as much personal disaster as anyone else. The difference is that we are held. The manager of Liverpool football team, Jürgen Klopp, once said in an interview:

'If anyone asks me about my faith, I give information. Not because I have claim to be any sort of missionary. But when I look at me and my life – and I take time for that every day – then I feel I am in sensationally good hands.'[21]

Most of us will have seen a squirrel gathering itself, high up at the end of a branch, and then leaping into space, reaching and stretching for the tree beyond. When it's in the air, it's both gloriously free and utterly vulnerable. It's also undeniably being itself. That's the kind of freedom and authenticity the leap of faith gives us. In faith, we become most fully ourselves – free and vulnerable, flying through the space between imagined certainties, that liminal space where everything is yet to be discovered and life is a wonderful possibility.

In *The Wind in the Willows* the following exchange occurs between the Mole and the Rat:

'So this is a River!' [says the Mole] 'THE River,' corrected the Rat. 'And you really live by the river?' 'By it, and with it, and on it, and in it,' said the Rat. 'It's brother and sister to me, and aunts, and company, and food and drink, and (naturally) washing. It's my world, and I don't want any other. What it hasn't got isn't worth having and what it doesn't know isn't worth knowing.'[22]

It's my world. That's what Bartimaeus discovered about faith the day he met Jesus; that it could become his world. When Jesus asked him that crucial question, 'What do you want me to do for you?' he answered simply, 'I want to see again.'

And he did. He saw a whole new world.

To ponder

- What would you like to think happened to Bartimaeus after this?
- How would you answer Jesus' question, 'What do you want me to do for you?'
- I wonder if you could say that faith is your world?

Prayer

A is for intercession; B is more contemplative.

A Pray for anyone you know who's blind or partially sighted, and
   for the work of the RNIB.
B Let Jesus ask you that question: 'What do you want me to do for
   you?' Answer it, telling Jesus both what you feel and what you
   need. Listen to your heart.

11

'Which of these three, do you think, was a neighbour to the man who fell into the hands of the robbers?' Luke 10.36 (25–37)

If I'm honest, I'm not altogether pleased with myself. I'm a lawyer, I ask questions, but I know that this time I'm not really asking an honest question. I want to catch him out.

You see, my people are getting worried. Even saying 'my people' makes me sound a bit seedy, but we think this Jesus has an agenda and we're not happy about it.

Sometimes he sounds like a fresh voice teaching about God and what God requires, but on other occasions he sounds as if he's actually undermining the law and challenging the authority of our teachers.

The problem is, he's very persuasive. He has presence. He's articulate, fluent; he tells great stories, he paints a seductive picture of God's plan, not just for the Jewish people but also for all people. He's saying that the promised age to come isn't just for Israel, that God's grace reaches way beyond the chosen people. And the lower classes get carried away with all this. We just don't know where it's all going to end.

So I'm here to put him on the spot and get him to admit that his ideas are actually heretical. Then people will see how dangerous he is. It's my duty as a lawyer to challenge and expose him.

He's talking with his friends, who seem to have been away for a while, so he's catching up. A crowd has gathered as well, which they say always happens when he arrives, so it's time for me to stand up and make my bid.

'Teacher,' I say, 'what must I do to inherit eternal life?'

Now, I know the answer to this, and I'm sure that he knows I know. So he comes straight back at me and asks what I think, what do I see written in the law? I give him the answer any educated Jew would give: we have to love God with everything we've got – our heart, soul, mind and strength, and our neighbour too. He approves, of course. It's the answer we both know. 'Do this, and you'll live,' he says.

So now I come back with my follow-up question, all innocent, really keen to know . . .

'And who is my neighbour?'

This is where we catch him. Either he stays this side of the line and says we have to look after our friends in the faith of our fathers or he steps over the line and says that our duty is also to foreigners and strangers and whoever else he includes in his wild teaching.

We look at each other. Me, wide-eyed and innocent; he, deciding what to say. A smile begins to play around his lips, his eyes sparkle and he starts to tell a story.

'A man was going down from Jerusalem to Jericho,' he begins, 'and he fell into the hands of robbers.' Well, we can all imagine that. It's a dangerous road. It drops 3,000 feet in just a few miles, twisting its way down through rocky desert, giving robbers far too many hiding places. So this lone traveller is an easy target and gets thoroughly beaten up, the robbers leaving him half dead. Then along comes a priest who, quite correctly, leaves him alone. If the man was dead, the priest would be contaminated by touching the corpse. Indeed, the body could have been planted there by the robbers so that they could do even more damage, by attacking another passing traveller.

Then a Levite came along, a Temple assistant, and he did the same. He couldn't know whether the battered body had any life in it or not, and he too would have been disqualified from his Temple responsibilities if the man had been dead and he touched him.

'Which of these three, do you think, was a neighbour?'

It's all perfectly reasonable and Jesus is telling the story well, but then he starts to go off in a weird direction.

He introduces a Samaritan.

Now, Samaritans are the sworn enemies of any self-respecting Jew. They come from the population of the northern hill country – people who, stupidly, mixed with foreigners after the Assyrians overran them centuries ago. They didn't want the Temple rebuilt in Jerusalem and put up their own special place on Mount Gerizim instead. They're completely out of order, these Samaritans, and we keep well away from one another.

But to my horror, and the amazement of the other people here, Jesus goes on to describe in his story how this heretic, this enemy of all right-thinking Jews, took care of the victim on the road and carted him back to an inn, stayed overnight to look after him, then left money for his continuing care when he had to leave the next day. Why would he do that? He was a Samaritan!

I'm still coming to terms with this bizarre tale, which breaks every rule in the book, when Jesus fixes me with a firm, clear gaze. 'Which of these three, do you think, was a neighbour to the man who fell into the hands of the robbers?' he asked me.

I'm caught. I know what I want to say, but I can't. I'd like to say that the Samaritan can't be a neighbour to any of us – it's not allowed – but I have to say what I really don't want to say: 'The one who showed him mercy – the Samaritan.'

The Samaritan.

What have I said? That people like this, our enemies, could be our neighbours? We should care for them and let them care for us? It can't be right. How come I have been trapped like this?

Then, to complete my embarrassment, Jesus says to me – earnestly, not triumphantly – 'Go and do the same.'

What on earth can I say to my people?

• • •

'Which of these was a neighbour to the man who fell into the hands of robbers?' The question has rung through the centuries and quickened the conscience of millions of believers and non-believers

79

alike. The lawyer's question has also rung loudly: 'And who is my neighbour?' We have all probably felt the force of that question.

Of course, Jesus changed the question. He was asked, 'Who is my neighbour?' and he answered, 'Who proved to *be* a neighbour?' But it doesn't matter. It's what Jesus did so often: he got people to rethink their prejudices, to turn the kaleidoscope round by 90 or even 180 degrees to see how the pattern can then fall in a quite different way.

In this case, the nice, tidy expectation that it is neighbours who belong to God's chosen people, was reframed by Jesus as *there are no boundaries to those who may count as our neighbours*. Abandon status, privilege and exclusiveness; we're all neighbours to one another in the kingdom of God.

Who do you regard as a neighbour? Do you have limits? How do you handle the flood of worthy causes that pours in daily via social media feeds, news broadcasts and unsolicited mail? What is Jesus asking you to do?

I was once walking with a friend to a train station in what we thought was a safe district of Cape Town (near Newlands cricket ground, which made me feel extra safe – who would do anything nasty near one of the world's most beautiful cricket grounds?). A young black man came up to us and asked if we were all right, because the district we were in was quite dangerous. He asked if he could take us safely to a different station on the same line. That put us on the alert – we wondered if we were actually being led into even more danger by this man – but he turned out to be as good as his word and we arrived at the station safely. We were not left at the side of the road, half dead. This was a good Samaritan from a different culture who had nothing to gain personally by helping two strangers, but he did it anyway.

Let's sharpen our analysis of this story a bit more. Jesus was saying that it's not sufficient to be a decent human being, prepared to help another person in need. Rather, we have to realize that loving our neighbour might require us to love our *enemy* – as in this case (Samaritans and Israelites were enemies). We can't restrict the meaning of the word 'neighbour'.

'Which of these three, do you think, was a neighbour?'

This is quite challenging. Most of us have an image of ourselves as essentially good people doing our best. We look after ourselves, our loved ones and our friends, and we would gladly help any others we came across who were in need if we had the time, skill and capacity. All very civilized. Jesus, though, stretches this cosy, self-satisfied decency to breaking point. There should be no limits to the territory of our concern when it comes to loving our neighbour, he says.

So how does this work? It seems that there are no boundaries in terms of those I should care for and whose care I should accept. What about sex offenders who rape little girls or terrorists who destroy innocent lives in city centres? Those are two of my problem categories. When I was visiting a prison once, I was offered tea and cake by the female half of a couple convicted of being serial killers. How did I feel about that? Confused.

However, Jesus is insistent. Love doesn't have boundaries. It includes the rejects, the marginalized, the poor, the overlooked, the lost, the ostracized, those beyond the pale. We can't leave anyone by the roadside half dead.

He drew a circle that shut him out,
heretic, rebel, a thing to flout.
But Love and I had the wit to win.
We drew a circle that took him in.[23]

But does this imply that we have to be soft on 'enemies' who do appalling things? Does it imply condoning evil or relativizing it? Surely it mustn't. Evil has to be named and not excused. Anger at the sex offender and the terrorist is absolutely understandable and acceptable; it's also *necessary* if we're to keep our moral lens clear. A God who doesn't judge between good and evil doesn't really care. Judging evil isn't the opposite of love; it's the expression of it. So how are we to reconcile this with God's extraordinary love and acceptance?

Richard Harries gives the illustration of a mother's love for her son who's in prison for a series of damaging and hurtful crimes he committed to feed his drug habit. She's angry with him for what he's done and how he's hurt so many people, but she doesn't stop loving him.

> What brings at-one-ment between the mother and her son? She doesn't have to change her attitude. She loves him and will continue to do so. It's he who has to change. He expresses his deep remorse and sorrow, and mother and son embrace in tears of sadness and joy. What has happened to her anger? It is somehow dissolved in the mutual tears and joy of mother and son. It is not as though everything is forgotten, but it's no longer on her mind and she certainly doesn't bring it up in conversation. So it is with God and us.[24]

We have to see the person who has done wrong – even outrageous wrong – as a neighbour, not excusing or minimizing the evil but, rather, seeing it absorbed by the cross, where all evil is gathered up and loaded on to God. Anger is absolutely appropriate, but even anger can be transformed at the cross.

One of the most demanding imperatives of the Christian life is to see everyone who crosses our path as an embodiment of Christ. It's spelt out in Matthew 25.40: 'Just as you did it to one of the least of these . . . you did it to me.' It's restated beautifully in the Rule of St Benedict, chapter 53: 'All guests who present themselves are to be welcomed as Christ.' That's a huge expectation, but Christ keeps presenting himself.

It's often said that Christian faith is a verb more than a noun. It's active. Love of neighbour is something that we *do*. Indeed, it's often easier to do it than to feel it. We're very fond of words in our faith and practice. We define, organize, argue, plan, pray. We prepare reports, pass resolutions and create procedures. We use an inordinate number of words in our worship. I sometimes think that God must get irritated by all the time we take telling him who he is instead of trying to hear what he wants and doing it.

Reflecting on Jesus' hard-hitting parable in Matthew 25, where Jesus challenges us on our response to the naked, the hungry and thirsty, the stranger, the sick and the prisoner, Sam Wells writes:

'Which of these three, do you think, was a neighbour?'

'When did we see you naked?' is a question that echoes through our consciences. Jesus was naked on the day of crucifixion. He was hungry and thirsty on that day too. Hence his cry, 'I thirst.' Jesus was also a stranger. Hence his words, 'He came to what was his own, and his own people did not accept him.' He was sick – in Gethsemane his sweat became like drops of blood falling down to the ground. And he was led away to prison after Judas' kiss. On each occasion his people failed to be with him. And the irony of the six great acts of mercy is their simplicity. Give food, give a drink, welcome, clothe, care, visit. Not end famine, heal disease, solve the refugee crisis: just the simple encounter that requires face-to-face meeting, without a solution or a cure or even a panacea to hand.[25]

Just do it.

The most distinctive Christian act is to love – love God, our neighbour and our enemy. The New Testament book is not called the Thoughts of the Apostles or the Discussions of the Apostles, but the Acts of the Apostles. The tactics take a lifetime of trial and error, but the strategy is clear. It's a call to action, across the widest of canvases. To love beyond the boundaries of convention and reason. To love for love's sake, for the One who is Love and is lovingly present with all people without exception.

Rabbi Lionel Blue spoke for his own Jewish faith and also for Christians when he said, 'Do something for the sake of heaven, and heaven happens.'

'Which of these three, do you think, was a neighbour to the man who fell into the hands of the robbers?'

The one who did something – and without asking if he was 'one of us'.

To ponder

- What has been your most vivid experience of being helped unexpectedly by a good Samaritan?
- Who are the people with whom you have most difficulty? How might you include them in the 'circle that took him in'.

'Which of these three, do you think, was a neighbour?'

- How would you answer the three questions put by St Ignatius in his Spiritual Exercises?
  - What have I done for Christ?
  - What am I doing for Christ?
  - What am I going to do for Christ?

Prayer

A is for intercession; B is more contemplative.

A Pray for any people who may unintentionally be made to feel like 'outsiders' in your church. Pray for their full inclusion. Pray, too, for those who are made to feel like outsiders in society – migrants, people who experience exclusion because of race, religion, sexuality or disability.

B Think through the last day and remember some of the people you've seen and perhaps not really valued – shop staff, refuse collectors, newsreaders. Ask God to speak to you about these groups of people or about individuals you might not be noticing and valuing.

12

'Has no one condemned you?'
John 8.10 (1–11)

It's the most embarrassing moment of my life. I know it's wrong, he knows it's wrong, but I've known this friend since our first day at school, and my marriage has been brutal, so it feels a bit different.

At first, he just listened; he was such a good listener and I had such a lot to pour out. Then, when I was sobbing with pain, he would put his arm round my shoulders. Then, well, one thing led to another . . . and now, here we are, caught at the most vulnerable moment imaginable. I won't go into details, but let's just say, we weren't wearing many clothes . . .

The way they came in, though – the purity police! Those Pharisees think they're so righteous. All pomposity and mock horror. All right, it isn't their fault – they feel that they have to do it to uphold the best interests of the law before God – but they were so lascivious, so uptight, so vengeful.

At first, I was hysterical. Now, I'm just resigned to the situation. I know what it means. I saw it once. Grown men throwing rocks at a poor woman, caught like me. They were in a frenzy, even as one rock after another crashed into her beautiful face, her frail body, the back of her head. Blood everywhere. It was unbelievable. I ran round the corner and vomited.

They throw me some clothes. I struggle into a kind of decency as they leer at me. Then they drag me off. It's unreal. A moment ago, I was in another world of joy and release, warmth, security and the madness of love. Then, in an instant, I was torn away from him, my Samuel . . . and now face the prospect of being stoned.

They drag me off to some place in the Temple precincts. I stumble along in a daze. This can't be happening. People watch, guess my shame. Some spit at me. Finally, they shove me roughly to the ground, near the feet of someone I've never seen before. A man, sitting on a stone bench, talking with a group of friends or teaching them – I don't know which. It doesn't matter.

My accusers start speaking to the man, full of self-righteousness and oily words. I feel somehow that I'm caught in a bigger game here, a useful victim, a test case. Where's Samuel? Has he been let off? Of course I hope so, but it's strange that I'm the only one to be sacrificed.

They tell the man what's happened, and the way they tell it sounds so awful, nothing like our experience of love. My mother would understand. Not approve, but understand. I want her. I want her so much.

'So what do you say, teacher?' They spit out the last word. 'The law says death by stoning. Isn't that right?' The taunt hangs in the air.

I'm face down on the ground, my eyes staring at the sand and dirt. A small spider stops in its tracks, then hurries off to safety. It has more chance of being alive tomorrow than I do. I listen to the silence above me as my life hangs in the balance.

I wait. The sun beats down, but I'm shivering. I risk a sideways glance at the man whose feet I'm getting to know quite well and – this is really odd – he seems to be drawing in the sand with his finger! For a bizarre moment I'm curious about what he's drawing. For heaven's sake, what does it matter? I pull myself together.

It seems somehow as if the man is refusing to play the game the purity police want. Strangely, I like this man, even though, at any moment, he might condemn me to a terrible death. They get more excited, more self-righteous. They repeat the charge and the question. 'Is it right to stone her to death?' It's almost an incantation. I disappear even deeper into myself.

Mother, please come and find me. Hold me like you used to . . .

Then the man seems to wake up from his reverie. He straightens his back and I risk another look. Is this it? Is this my death sentence? His eyes are hard as they survey my tormentors. I realize that he's controlling himself with great difficulty because, in fact, he's angry. His voice, however, is firm and clear.

'All right,' he says. 'Whoever here has never committed a sin, whoever here is sinless in his own eyes, you be the first person to throw a stone at this woman.'

Then he just sits down and continues to draw in the sand! It's extraordinary. I push myself up on an elbow, shaking my head to make sure that I've heard him right. The man carries on drawing.

Silence. Except for the laughter of children playing over the wall. The shouts of street sellers. Raised voices from a distant argument.

Then (I can't believe it's happening), one of the most senior Pharisees turns and slips away quietly. After a few awkward seconds, another does the same. Then another. And then it seems that they all know the game's up and they drift off, disappointment and defeat hanging over them as they creep away.

I realize that I've been holding my breath. I kneel up, as carefully and quietly as I can. I keep still. I know I'm guilty and so does the man who's saved me. I assume nothing, and wait.

Then this lovely, gracious man asks the most astonishing thing. He says to me, very gently, 'Has no one condemned you?' I shake my head tentatively, afraid to believe. 'No sir,' I manage to say. 'No one.' We look at each other, a world of conversation unsaid.

Then words I'll always remember: 'I don't condemn you either,' he says, and I feel a huge weight slipping off my back. 'Go on your way now, but don't get caught up in the things that you know are wrong.'

A white dove chooses this moment to take off, carrying good news to heaven.

• • •

'Has no one condemned you?' Can we hear that liberating question addressed to us? It's important. It goes to the heart of the gospel. It's not that Jesus is a soft touch, prepared to let anything go. After all, he said clearly to the woman, 'Don't sin again.' (And the way he laid into

87

the hypocrisy of the Pharisees on occasions was scary – see Matthew 23.) But he knows that we often carry around enough self-imposed guilt and shame already, without any more being loaded on to us by others. After all, we have a view from the front stalls; we know precisely what we do when no one's looking and, worse, we know what we're *thinking*. What we need most often isn't condemnation but a sense of perspective and the opportunity to get back on the road.

I'm pretty clear about my darknesses. I'd rather do without public humiliation and someone to push my face even more firmly into the dust. I need someone to lift me out of that dust, to believe that I'm capable of being better. That's what Jesus did for the unnamed woman that day. He said, in effect, 'I believe you can be better than this.'

'Has no one condemned you?' We should listen to that liberating question, but the sad truth is, many people believe God does actually condemn them. Lurking at the back of their minds (often not admitted) is an image of God as a disapproving parent, a cosmic policeman, a stern judge who's waiting to catch them out. I remember, in my teenage years, being vaguely aware of a great cosmic ledger, in which were recorded my successes and failures in trying to live a 'good' life. The image hung around, no matter how firmly my rational mind rejected it. The sad result of this picture of God can be a faith that's concerned with control and conformity rather than life in abundance (John 10.10). The Church becomes a sin-management organization rather than a life-giving movement.

So what's going on? Why is that image of God so common? Particularly as the Bible is insistent that God's nature is love, top to bottom, front and centre.

It might help to think of it this way. Imagine a field, open to the nourishment and refreshment of sun and rain, but in one corner, someone has dumped toxic chemicals. As the rain falls on to the field, it carries those chemicals into the soil, so what was pure rain changes into something much more noxious and unpleasant when it's absorbed into the ground. In a similar way, we might see the pure love of God forever falling on the field of humanity, but being changed by the fallenness of our human nature and that of the world, so we end up *experiencing* that love as blame, even though that's not at all its true nature. In fact, it's the 'toxic chemicals', both in and around us, that distort our perception of the 'pure rain' of God's love.

To think of it another way, although my memory is that I only really lost my temper once with our daughters (they might remember differently, of course), what that daughter might have experienced as irrational parental anger was actually wounded love. How could this have happened between us? But never for a moment did I stop loving my daughter – I love her with an everlasting love.

Julian of Norwich, the fourteenth-century mystic, wrote:

> God looks on human sinfulness and brokenness with pity and not with blame . . . By the same judgement I understood that sinners sometimes *deserve* blame and wrath [but] I could not see these two in God.[26]

In other words, it's *our* perception that leads us to experience God as judgemental, but that's not the reality. Our false perception is caused by a combination of various distortions – poor parenting, poverty, lack of education, accidents, genes, life chances – together with our own bad choices, of course. All such factors distort our perception of God and life generally. The reality is, however, that God's consistent message to us is one of love and forgiveness. 'Has no one condemned you? Neither do I.'

The fact is, we all have to face up to problematic aspects of our behaviour. Mother Mary Clare of the Sisters of the Love of God wrote, 'My prayer is really one sentence: "Here I am, what a mess."' Having such honesty is a great release as we come before God. Let's not pretend. After all, we've not got it all sorted, we're not what we want to be, we're still a mass of mistakes, muddles, obsessions and fears. If we try to hide the messy, unacceptable parts of our personality from God, he won't be able to work with us to transform us into the likeness of Christ. For our part, honesty opens us up to receiving the breathtaking grace of God: a love beyond belief. A love that doesn't condemn.

Radical American Lutheran pastor Nadia Bolz-Weber was always likely to find conventional church difficult. As a student she was once hauled up before a church bureaucrat who seemed to be threatening that she wouldn't be ordained unless she learned to express herself more sensitively. She was angry and phoned a good friend. She exploded, saying:

'How dare he? Is he really going to stop me from doing this church thing just because he doesn't think pastors should use the word "bullshit"? Give me a f*****g break.' I was in full-on rage mode, which I now know is usually a cover for when I'm full-on scared. He talked me down, but not all the way. Before he hung up he said 'I love you Nadia.' It broke something in me . . . To hear I was loved meant something very particular because of the context in which I heard it, as though he was saying, 'You are a mess, and you are loved. You have a little issue with anger, and you are loved. I've not even known you that long, [but] you are loved. You think you're going through this alone, but you are wrong, and you are loved. The thing you are experiencing right now seems so big, but what is bigger is that you are loved.'[27]

The woman in John's Gospel heard that same message: you are loved. It meant everything.

In the 1960s, theologian Paul Tillich delighted a generation of Christians with his way of expressing the heart of the Christian faith. He maintained that the gospel meant we could 'accept that we are accepted, even though unacceptable'. It was typical existentialist 1960s language, but it was a way to state succinctly what Jesus was saying to the woman taken in adultery. He *accepted* her gladly and fully: 'Neither do I condemn you.' Just *accept* that gift, he said – 'Go your way' – but drop the *unacceptable* behaviour: 'don't sin again'. Perhaps we all need to hear that afresh. Accept that you are accepted, even though it may seem to you that you're unacceptable.

Or, more simply, 'Has no one condemned you?'

To ponder

- Do you sometimes, deep down, think of God as a disapproving parent or did you think that at one time?
- How do you respond to Julian of Norwich saying that God looks at us with pity, not with blame? Is that enough?
- I wonder if you like, or agree with, Tillich's way of understanding the gospel, that we need to 'accept that we are accepted, even though unacceptable'?

Prayer

A is for intercession; B is more contemplative.

A Pray for those who have been condemned, either justly (convicted criminals) or unjustly (political prisoners or pawns in international disputes). Pray also for our criminal justice system and for the work of Amnesty International.

B Allow yourself to be held in the compassionate gaze of Christ. Let his kindly gaze rest on you and stay with you. Return to that gaze throughout the day and be reassured that Christ is with you and you are loved.

13

'Whose head is this, and whose title?'
Mark 12.16 (13-17)

Here we go again. Another group of slimy religious types trying to catch Jesus out. You'd have thought they'd have known better by now. They tried to get him on divorce a few days ago, then yesterday, they pitched up to ask where his authority came from. I wonder what it'll be this time?

I'm on duty with Jesus today. We don't all go with him every day when he teaches in the Temple precincts. We're not all needed, but we like to keep an eye on him and prevent him from being overwhelmed by an overenthusiastic crowd – or, in the back of our minds, being attacked by a random fanatic or zealous Temple police. Jesus doesn't see the need for this kind of support; he's such a free spirit, he's a danger to himself sometimes. He'd prefer us to be meeting friends in the city and sharing our experiences with them rather than seemingly making a fuss about his personal safety.

Right now, he's in full flow and, let's face it, it has to be him who's talking about the kingdom of God here in the Temple itself. Way back in the early days, he sent us out into the villages around Galilee and got us preaching and healing on his behalf, as it were. It was really scary. Most of us thought that we were hopeless, but God still seemed to use our faltering attempts to do what Jesus asked – to preach about the kingdom and – would you believe it? – to heal people who were sick! We came back full of it. I guess Jesus was right: the best way to learn about mission is to go on mission. Just like the best way to learn about prayer is by praying.

Anyway, now it's just Jesus doing the teaching and he's taking the good news about the kingdom right into the heart of Jewish life and faith, the Temple itself. If people are going to 'get it' they've got to get it here. Jesus is bringing fresh air to the old traditions. He makes some sparkle again and others he turns upside down. When he talks about the kingdom he seems to shine; it's as if sunlight is pouring out of him. But there's also a sense for some of us that darkness is spilling out on to the streets and we're walking into a trap.

You can see a bit of that darkness right now, with this creepy group coming over to talk. By the way they're dressed and the way they talk, I think it's a mix of Pharisees and Herodians – that lot who, for some reason, support Herod's nasty dynasty and, in particular, Herod Antipas, who throws his weight about in Galilee. I suppose the Herodians have come to Jerusalem for the festival. Rumour has it Antipas is here as well.

So here they are, all smiley and smarmy. 'Jesus,' they say, 'it's great to see you here, helping us all to understand the law better. Thank you. We have a little problem, though, and we hope that you'll be good enough to help us.' I'm wincing already. 'We know you're a good man, Jesus. Sincere. We know that you teach the way of God without fear or favour. So this is our problem.' Smiles getting wider all the time. 'Should we pay taxes to Caesar or not?'

So *that's* it.

Oh, so innocent! How could these fine, upstanding, religious Jews be anything but honest seekers after truth, simply wanting to know the best way to live out their faith? How could we possibly think ill of them?

Of course, they're nothing of the sort. It's a deceitful little ploy. Let me explain how it works. Taxes are a very contentious subject for us Jews. We have to pay a local tax, depending on where we live. Then we have a Temple tax, to look after the great building itself and, presumably, line the pockets of the religious leaders along the way. But then we have this Roman tax too; we're expected to pay the expenses of our own oppressors! We really resent that because – think about it – if we pay taxes to someone, that's saying we accept their authority. We've had pretty much 500 years of being under someone else's authority and we're seriously hacked off with it. The Herodians are OK about the tax because they support the status quo. The Pharisees, by and large, go along with it, though they aren't particularly happy. Most of us just hate it.

So back to this 'innocent' little problem these poor religious people have got. Should they pay the tax or not? What does Jesus think? Big expectant smile.

As if we don't see the trap a mile off. If Jesus says to pay it, he's no friend of the people. If he says not to pay it, it'll be tantamount to inciting a revolt and that's a capital offence.

Even after my years of following Jesus around, these are the occasions that have me holding my breath. How will he get out of this one?

Oh me of little faith! Jesus doesn't hurry to answer. He's still sitting on the steps, relaxed. Waiting for his moment, he looks at them, level-eyed, serious, unworried. (I can do worry for both of us and a few more.) It's a look that says, 'I know you know that I know we all know what's going on here.' They look away.

'Let me see a denarius,' Jesus says.

Now that's an interesting move. The denarius is a particularly unpleasant symbol of our oppression. On one side is an image of the emperor. Around it are the words 'Augustus Tiberius, son of the divine Augustus'. On the other side it says 'High Priest', because emperors are routinely high priests of the main Roman cult. So in one fell swoop, the Romans utterly offend every faithful Jew. How can any man be divine? Only the one holy God of Abraham, Isaac and Jacob is divine. And how can he be a high priest? That isn't an emperor's job.

So this is the nasty little coin Jesus gets them to produce. 'Now,' he says, 'whose head is this, and whose title?' 'The emperor's,' they say, looking puzzled. Where is this going?

'Right,' says Jesus, looking them straight in the eye. 'Give to the emperor what belongs to him and to God what belongs to God.'

Brilliant! Demolished in one short sentence. None of us saw it coming. 'Give to Caesar what belongs to him.' He said it contemptuously – kind of, 'Send the filthy stuff back where it came from. I'm not interested in that.' Then his devastating final line, 'But give to God what belongs to God', which is everything! We owe everything to God, our very lives. God is our absolute priority every time. Our scriptures tell us – and Jesus keeps reminding us – that we're made in the image of God, so if that dirty little coin with the image of the emperor belongs to him, then we, with the image of God, belong to the most high and holy One.

They look shocked. One of them starts to stammer something in reply, but he dries up after a few words. There's no way back. They shuffle away, looking distinctly fed up.

Jesus carries on teaching, picking up where he left off.

How does he do it? Does he think these things up in quiet moments in the evening so that he's ready for these challenges or do they just pop into his quicksilver mind? Whichever it is, I'm amazed and thrilled.

'Whose head is this, and whose title?' I must remember that tonight, when the lads ask how it went today.

Brilliant. Just brilliant.

. . .

Brilliant, yes; but open to misunderstanding. Tragically, this great response by Jesus to a sneaky trick question has often been used to justify splitting human life into two parts: the political/social and the spiritual/religious. That's a much later, eighteenth-century idea, but it has often been used to delegitimize Christian interrogation of particular political or national policies. Christian leaders are regularly told to 'keep out of politics', as if that were possible in a world which belongs to God but, at the same time, is seriously out of kilter with goodness, peace and justice.

Christian tradition has always set itself against such a, frankly, heretical view of the significance of this world in the eyes of God

– heretical because it flies in the face of a basic theological conviction about the nature of humanity being made in God's image. We are not disembodied spirits but embodied persons whose flourishing involves not just sustenance of the spirit but also adequacy of housing and education, employment, food and water supply, health and legal protection. Gandhi said that those who believe religion and politics aren't connected don't understand either. Desmond Tutu is equally clear: 'I am puzzled about which Bible people are reading when they suggest that religion and politics don't mix.'

Is there part of you that isn't convinced? Is there a bit of you that thinks bishops shouldn't get involved in social and political issues?

There are two particular potholes for Christians to look out for. One is to be theoretically committed to social and political change, but underplay its importance in practice. In my early years as a Christian, I would speak positively about the need for Christian engagement in issues of poverty, inequality, racism and so on, but it took my exposure to the realities of those issues in the centre of Birmingham to raise my political temperature above lukewarm. The needs of the homeless around the Bullring shopping centre, the loneliness of the high-rise flats, the demonic hold of addictions, the basic needs of the world's poor – these all bore down on me in a new way. 'Where would Jesus be?' was my constant question.

Rabbi Jonathan Sacks wrote of:

the cognitive dissonance between the world that is, and the world that ought to be. *The only way of resolving this dissonance is a deed.* That is the difference between faith-as-acceptance and faith-as-protest. The only way to deal with slavery is to lead the people to freedom. The only way to confront the evils of the *polis* [state] is to build a more just social order.[28] (My italics.)

We do need more than theoretical agreement on these issues of justice, equity and human flourishing; we need a deed. Martin Luther King Jr undertook more such deeds in a few years than most people could achieve in several lifetimes. He said that there were 'some things within our social order to which I'm proud to be maladjusted', and he went on to name segregation and discrimination, religious bigotry, poverty, militarism and more. With a characteristic rhetorical flourish, he called for a new organization – the International Association for the Advancement of Creative Maladjustment.[29]

The other possible pothole is to confuse political and social action with the policies of particular parties. Christians have no business claiming a religious or biblical mandate for a party that is either in government or in opposition. We will inevitably read the evidence of their policies personally and come to different conclusions, but we can't claim the religious high ground for our own reading either. A British diplomat once quipped, 'Capitalism is the exploitation of man by man. Communism is the other way round.' Extremes of both right and left are rarely attractive. What matters is not what's right and what's left, but what's right and what's wrong.

The biblical material on how we should relate to the state as people of faith is not straightforward. The advice in Romans 13 is a world away from the situation envisaged in Revelation 13, for example. In Romans, we are encouraged to be subject to the governing authorities, because they have been instituted by God and can therefore claim our qualified loyalty. In Revelation, the state (the Beast) is shown to be seeking unconditional loyalty from its subjects and thereby has become demonic – which was the case in Nazi Germany and the former Soviet Union.

The witness of the Bible as a whole, however, is that ultimate loyalty belongs only to God: 'Give to God the things that are God's.' Our loyalty to God needs to be the fount from which all our decisions flow. In the last resort, it has led people of peace to take part in plots to assassinate heads of state (Bonhoeffer with Hitler) and, in other cases, to be conscientious objectors, showing phenomenal courage in war situations (Desmond Doss, Hacksaw Ridge). In the early Church, Christians died appalling deaths rather than say that the emperor was Lord when, to them, only Jesus was Lord. In sixteenth-century Japan, Christians bled to death in the torture of what was called the Pit rather than forsake their ultimate loyalty to God. In 1886, King Mwanga of Buganda burnt to death 32 young Christians who wouldn't renounce their faith, and they went to their death singing. As did 20 Egyptian Coptic Christians beheaded by Daesh on a Libyan beach in 2015.

It was the same loyalty that led a first-century Palestinian Jew to say that his hearers should give to the emperor what belonged to the emperor, as long as they gave to God what belonged to God. He paid the price with his life.

'Whose image is this?' If we were to think of Jesus' question being addressed to us, what we'd hear would be Jesus asking us who we really think that we belong to. If we belong to God and bear his image, that is a full-time job. There's no part of our lives that doesn't belong to him. If our lives are pointed towards God as the true north of our existence, then we need to scan through all 360 degrees to assess which parts of our lives are truly in God's hands and which aren't.

Going to church and praying during the week is certainly in God's hands. Giving some time to our church, a committee, perhaps, and some money ('within reason', we think) – yes, that too – but where do we go after that? Do we include our attitude to our neighbour, the *Big Issue* seller, our closest relationships (which often pose the biggest challenges)? Do we bring our work, our obsessions, our sexuality, our use of time, the people we haven't forgiven, the ideals that we put aside for another day? If we bear the image of God and God has our ultimate loyalty, we're likely to need to reorder a good deal of the conduct of our daily lives. Not to make us excessively pious and religious, but to make us more deeply Christian.

Jesus doesn't harangue us about it. He simply asks, 'Whose image do you carry?'

To ponder

- I wonder if Jesus enjoyed winding people up?
- What has your ultimate loyalty? (Think broadly about that one.)
- How much is your faith reflected in your political thinking?
- What areas of your life don't yet really belong to God?

Prayer

A is for intercession; B is more contemplative.

A Pray by name for Christians involved in political life locally or nationally. Perhaps, in your imagination, clothe one person in particular with the armour of God: the belt of truth, the breastplate of righteousness, the gospel of peace, the shield of faith, the helmet of salvation and the sword of the Spirit (Ephesians 6.10–17).

B Lay out a number of tealights and touch a flame to each one as you name a current concern in our national and international life. Imagine the light gradually suffusing those situations with hope. There's no need for words; just let the candles shine.

14

'Do you know what I have done to you?'
John 13.12 (1–20)

It's good to have a meal together tonight. It's Thursday night, Passover tomorrow, but we've been spread round the city for most of the week, catching up with friends, telling them about Jesus, and only a few of us have been with Jesus each day while he's been teaching in the Temple precincts.

Mind you, he's been a bit of a celebrity there. The top lawyers have been out in force, trying to catch him out with clever questions, and he's wrong-footed them every time. But I have to admit, it's tiring out there. The city is seething, what with it being our biggest festival and people pouring in from all over the countryside and beyond. The soldiers are here, too, keeping more than an eye on us. It's all a bit overwhelming for those of us more used to the shoreline of Galilee. Already I'm longing for that great expanse of sky, the distant call of fishermen, the familiar outline of hills across the water.

Anyway, we're here again, eating well, telling stories, friendly banter up and down the table. It's a nice room – plain but well prepared, candles casting a warm glow over the whole scene. I see alert, friendly, weather-beaten faces and good food – bread and olives, meats and cheese, humous and fruits, plus goblets of red wine. I can feel myself gradually relaxing after the tension of the city streets. These are some of the best times for me. We've had a busy day; we come in after dealing with all the crowds of people, hungry to get close to Jesus, and now, at last, we can wind down, just us, friends together, chat over the day, pressure off.

I'm next to Jesus; it often seems to happen that way. I know that he loves all of us, but it does seem as though he and I understand each other in a special way. Sorry, that sounds wrong. I'm out of my depth with Jesus – he's too deep, too fast, too intuitive, too intelligent for me – but we connect at some emotional level and I treasure that, and honour it.

Quietly, I try to guard his back.

So, all is going well.

Suddenly (and I really had no sense that this was going to happen), I see Jesus get up, take off his outer robe and put a towel round his waist, just like a servant. The room falls silent as others see what's happening too, and the last story fades away. Jesus fetches a bowl of water. Then we watch, hypnotized, as he starts to wash our feet!

Now, if you don't know about this practice, when we come in, our feet dusty and dirty after a day walking along the paths and alleyways in the city or the countryside, what we need is lots of water and a clean towel. In the better parts of town you have servants to wash your feet for you – not men, of course, but women, children or foreigners. So for Jesus himself, our leader, teacher, master, to do this for us – well, it's unthinkable. Sometimes a rabbi might have his disciples wash his feet, but never the other way round. What on earth is going on?

Stunned, we let it happen, in silence. Andrew, Matthew, Judas (he seems to take special care with Judas for some reason), then Philip, James and so on, round the low table. Then he gets to Simon Peter and – wouldn't you know it? – that's when the bubble bursts. Simon can't take it any more. 'Are you serious, Jesus?' he asks, obviously horrified. 'You really want to wash my feet?' Jesus sits back on his haunches and looks at his brave, troubled friend. 'Well, if I don't do it, you can't be part of me and what I'm here for,' he says. Simon is shocked by that one, but he manages to pull himself together. 'In that case, Lord, wash me all over, top to toe.' He's an all-or-nothing man is Simon.

Eventually, Jesus has finished. He goes back to his place, lies down again, propped up on one elbow, and says, in that way he has that really makes you want to listen:

101

'Do you know what I've done to you?'

He lets the question hang in the air, but we can tell that he's not expecting an answer. Do we know what he's done to us? Well, yes and no. We know that he's just done one of his extraordinary reversals again, where he takes what you think you know and understand and turns it on its head. He does that a lot in his teaching about the law, about what God really values in people, what the Temple is for, who really understands what's at stake and who's blind to it and so on. So, here we are again. This time the 'upside downness' is the important leader serving the ordinary followers. You've got to admit it's different!

But do we know what he's done to us beyond that? I don't think so. In fact, he said as much to Simon when he was protesting about being washed by Jesus. 'You don't understand what I'm doing now, but you will understand later.' As usual I end up feeling like I've hardly got one foot on the ladder. And I don't think I'm especially stupid.

But he goes on to explain. 'Listen,' he says, 'you call me your teacher and that's fine, because that's what I am. So if I, your teacher, have washed your feet, you also ought to wash one another's feet.' When he says that, it sounds so obvious, but I'm trying to think how it works out. So Peter should come and wash my feet every evening, though maybe Nathanael on the Sabbath, yes? And I should make a special point of Judas's personal cleanliness and Andrew's calloused feet. Is that it? At the start of the week, we should have a group foot-wash, with everyone washing everyone else's feet? Bags I do Matthew, because I know he's ticklish . . .

'You should wash one another's feet.' It all sounds so far-fetched. It's not what Jewish men do.

Anyway, there isn't time to think about this question any more. Jesus looks like he's settling in for one of his seminars. We call them that sometimes, just to make him laugh, but tonight he looks serious. He wants us to concentrate because he has a lot to say. If anyone writes this down, he's going to need a lot of quills.

I settle down beside Jesus. He seems surprisingly tense tonight. What's going on? Now I think about it, he said something odd when he was washing our feet. 'You're clean, in a sense,' he said, 'though that doesn't apply to all of you . . .'

I didn't notice it at the time, but I knew something was niggling away. And that was it. What did he mean? One of us isn't (in his word) 'clean'?

Questions. So many questions. I'm beginning to feel uneasy about tonight. I can't help feeling that, beneath the surface, things are beginning to break down.

• • •

The humility of Jesus is astonishing. What we see in the washing of feet is all of a piece with the one who was born in a borrowed stable, taught from a borrowed boat, fed 5,000 people with borrowed food, rode into Jerusalem on a borrowed donkey, celebrated the Last Supper in a borrowed room, borrowed the strength of a stranger to carry his cross and, finally, was buried in a borrowed tomb. Humility.

I sometimes wonder where we went wrong. For 20 years I have officially been titled 'The Right Reverend', sometimes referred to as 'Your Grace' and even 'My Lord'. Others are titled 'The Very Reverend' or even 'The Most Reverend'. How much further can we go? When you think of this official aggrandisement or the excesses of the medieval papacy, you can almost feel Jesus wince. Of course, this is what tends to happen when an idea becomes an institution – which it has to if it's to be passed on. But that doesn't mean we've got it right. It doesn't sit well with the penniless preacher from Galilee.

You can tell the whole story of Jesus in images, from a star and a stable to a cross and a tomb, but one of the most powerful images is that of a towel on the floor next to a bowl of dirty water. When I was a bishop in the Diocese of Durham, on the night before a new group of ordinands were to be set apart for ministry by ordination, there would be a moving ceremony in which everyone present would wash someone else's feet, and have theirs washed too. It was always as humbling to receive that tender care as it was to give it but, that night, it powerfully represented what was to be the heart of those ordinands' ministries.

True humility, after the pattern of Jesus, is obvious as soon as you see it. (As, sadly, is its opposite.) I once heard the former Bishop of Lichfield tell of a priest who had been consecrated bishop at short notice to go into South Sudan, where there was great need for wise oversight of the struggling Church. Nothing was heard of him for years, until finally he emerged, thin and worn but still faithful. It turned out that he had baptized hundreds of new Christians and there were now 50 new churches in the diocese. He was asked what he needed. 'Well,' he said, 'I'd like a new clerical shirt.'

The even deeper truth behind the humility of Jesus is the humility of God. This can be quite hard to take in. Have we come to terms with a God who washes feet? Can we accept that if Jesus gives us as true an image of God as it's possible to grasp, then God also kneels at our feet, looking for the opportunity to serve us – even us? It's crazy. The God of creation, of power and glory, the one who spins the stars, the magic in every molecule – this God is humble!

A belief in the importance of humility is one of the most astonishing changes Christianity brought to the lexicon of divinity in the early centuries. Humility was despised by pagan Greece and Rome. Aristotle saw it not as a virtue but as a vice – it was evidence of a lack of sincerity. Christianity turned this view upside down by proclaiming humility as one of the defining characteristics of virtue, and pride as the greatest vice.

The cultured despisers of religion have continued to belittle the virtue of humility throughout the ensuing centuries, and regularly confused it with being a doormat. Not at all! Humility requires that we have a proper respect for ourselves so that we are free enough to give ourselves away. Jesus was sure of his own identity and, consequently, able to surrender what the world counted as dignity but, to him, was irrelevant when put alongside the call to mutual service in the community that he was leaving behind. It was another glimpse of the freedom of Jesus, and the gift of freedom he came to give his followers. It was also a glimpse of the nature of God.

The logic, then, is that what is true of God was true of Jesus, and what was true of Jesus ought to be true of those who bear his name. So how does humility sit with us? Jesus asked his friends, 'Do you know what I have done to you?' It's the question we still have to take to heart, together with the subsequent instruction to do as he himself had demonstrated so memorably that message-laden night.

Western culture is full of hubris and self-regard. We're encouraged to polish our egos, exaggerate our CVs and sell ourselves hard on interview, so it's hard to inhabit the freedom of Jesus that enabled him to be humble. A man once asked his rabbi why people couldn't see the face of God any more. The rabbi answered, 'It seems that not many people can stoop that low.'

The humility that Jesus set before us in the washing of feet was the humility of mutual service among his followers, which should then be offered by those followers to the wider family of the world. There are few contexts today in which, theoretically, that mutuality is easier to practise than in the Church, given the extraordinary variety of people found in most congregations. This is where rich and poor, privileged and underprivileged, black and white, gay and straight, young and old, those with high educational achievements and those with none, all meet at a table where bread and wine are available and, ideally, a towel and a bowl are on the floor. Here, we serve one another, as Christ looks on. We haven't always learnt the lesson as well as we should have.

At a gathering when John Sentamu was Archbishop of York, he was asked by a little boy why he believed in God. The archbishop beckoned him to come to the front. Noticing the boy's shoelace was undone, he knelt down to retie it and said:

When I was a boy, someone told me that Jesus could be my friend. So, that night, I knelt by my bed and asked Jesus to be my friend. And do you know something? He still is my friend.[30]

You could have heard a pin drop.

What matters, however, isn't just an archbishop kneeling at a little boy's feet to tie his shoelace, nor the Archbishop of Canterbury in the pandemic volunteering as a chaplain in the hospital next to his flat in Lambeth Palace, nor Princess Diana memorably holding the hand of an AIDS patient. What really matters is the millions of acts of love performed daily throughout the world without pomp and circumstance or even a Twitter commentary. These things are done simply because that's what Jesus asked us to do, and that's what God is like.

'Do you know what I have done to you?' Yes and, however badly we do it, we're trying to copy that iconic action in all manner of ways – in this and this and this. Details of love that, one day, will cover the world.

To ponder

- I wonder how it would feel if you let Jesus wash your feet? Try to imagine it.
- Have you metaphorically washed someone else's feet? How did that feel?
- How do you feel about God, 'the Father Almighty', being humble?

Prayer

A is for intercession; B is more contemplative.

A Pray for the 'foot-washers' in society – nurses, care home staff, cleaners, workers with the homeless, those who clean our streets. Pray by name for any such people you know.

B If you can manage it, in your imagination let Jesus wash your feet. Thank him. Be amazed.

15

'Are you asleep?'
Mark 14.37 (32–42)

I'm embarrassed even to remember it. It was one of our lowest moments. As a group, we betrayed Jesus in a whole number of ways that night. Three of us went to sleep when he'd asked us to stay awake with him. Another one actually handed him over to the guards. Then, finally, we all ran away in a panic. Some friends we turned out to be! At the most critical time of his life, we all chose to save our own skins. We abandoned him.

The evening had started quite differently. We'd arrived for supper in high spirits after a day when Jesus' teaching in the Temple precincts had again held his listeners spellbound. Everywhere he spoke that week, people were stopped in their tracks. Of course, the people of Jerusalem always get excited in festival weeks, but Jesus' teaching about the kingdom of God bursting in right now and making the Temple kind of irrelevant – if not doomed – was making everyone sit up. We loved seeing the Pharisees huffing and puffing! So we were in a good mood as we gathered for this Passover meal.

But the atmosphere of the meal changed as it went on. A chill settled over the room. Jesus seemed strangely distracted and he spoke for a long time about pretty deep stuff. There was an awkward moment when he talked about one of us actually betraying him, but that seemed so off the wall I don't think we took it seriously. If only we had . . .

We shared what we call the 'bread of affliction' and the 'cup of redemption', as the Passover meal required, but Jesus described them as being like his own body and blood, which was a truly awful idea to us Jews; we'd never entertain the idea of drinking even an animal's blood, let alone a human's. He also said that he wouldn't drink wine like this again until he drank it fresh in the kingdom of God. It was all getting very heavy.

We went out into the still, suspicious night. It seemed as if calamity was in the air. Silently we straggled our way along the Kidron Valley, to the garden we often went to, the one owned by a friend of Jesus. Gethsemane, it's called, the place of the oil press.

Then Jesus took three of us aside, Peter, John and me. He did this occasionally. I used to think of Peter as a kind of warrior, the protector when anything looked as if it was going wrong. John was the thinker; you could see him absorbing everything and storing it away to reflect on later. I was just the follower, I suppose, learning how to live truthfully and honestly by watching how Jesus did it. I wanted to imitate him as much as I could. Anyway, he took the three of us aside and asked us to keep watch with him while he sorted some things out in prayer. Of course, we nodded, serious in our desire to help him.

How shallow, how weak we turned out to be! What miserable failures!

He walked away a little further among the olive trees and there sank to the ground to pray. He was clearly deadly serious. He seemed to be hammering something out with God, the One he'd taught us to call 'Abba'. We looked at one another in silence, aware of our responsibility, and found different bits of ground on which to make ourselves comfortable while we watched and waited.

But, oh, the shame of it! I don't know whether it was overtiredness, emotional exhaustion after that strange meal or simply having had too much to drink, but the next thing any of us knew, Jesus was standing over us, clearly disappointed. 'Are you asleep?' he asked softly. Actually, he addressed the question to Peter. Peter was probably put on the spot because he'd been so forthright (surprise, surprise) when Jesus said over supper that we'd all scatter like sheep when trouble came along, and Peter had sworn he'd never, ever, under any circumstances, betray Jesus.

'Are you asleep?' Yes, we were. Had we been asked expressly to keep watch with him in this critical time of prayer? Yes, we had. Did we have any excuse? No, we didn't.

We didn't know where to look.

Jesus looked sad. Then he said something I've always remembered: 'The spirit is willing, my young friends, but the flesh is weak.' It echoes in my dreams to this day. I now know how deep that goes.

He went away again to pray. The darkness seemed to close in on him as he sank down, stretching his whole body over a rock. It was the posture of a man in despair. Was Jesus falling apart? He seemed to be having a monumental struggle. In the light of what happened the next day, he must have been struggling with his Father, to see if there was any way of avoiding the catastrophe that was in store for him. It would have been a terrifying prospect for anyone, and it was truly alarming for us to watch as Jesus battled it out. We settled down again. This time we'd be faithful. This time.

So why was it that, again, Jesus found us asleep? Why? What was wrong with us? It was criminal to do it again. He didn't seem to blame us; he just looked alone, very alone. Again, we didn't know where to look, as he asked us to try, please, to stay with him. Just to stay with him. Surely that wasn't too much to ask?

I can hardly bring myself to own up to the next bit. I'll say it very softly: we fell asleep again. It's almost impossible to imagine, I know, but it's true. The next thing I remember is coming round with my mind in a fog, realizing with horror that I'd done it again, and beating myself up about it without mercy. Incredibly, Jesus was standing there, looking renewed in some way, and much more like his old self.

'All right,' he said. 'It's over. The hour we've been expecting has come at last. My betrayer is almost with us. Up you get, let's go.' He was speaking with authority again. The struggle had been resolved. The steel had come back. He knew what had to happen and, amazingly, he still wanted us, failures all, to come with him.

Looking back, I suppose that it was an ideal time and place for Judas. It was night, when dark deeds take place; we were outside the city, so there wouldn't be too many people to get in the way; and his friends were going to be drowsy after a big meal. Even so, for Judas to give him the kiss of friendship that turned out to be the kiss of death was an awful thing to see. It's hard to forgive Judas, though I'm sure Jesus did.

Our 'warrior' picked up a sword, of course (why wouldn't he?), but Jesus wasn't interested in last-minute acts of defiance. He handed himself over. There was something noble about the way he did it. He wasn't like a frightened victim. He was a free man, making his own choice.

But we weren't free. We were trapped both by the shame of our failure to stay awake when Jesus needed us most and by our humiliating fear of capture, torture or worse. We ran for our lives.

Still my dreams are haunted by that poignant question: 'Are you asleep?' I can't deny it – and I can't believe it – but there we are; it happened.

• • •

Are *we* asleep? Are those of us who call ourselves Christians asleep on the job? As figures for church attendance continue to slide downwards year on year, have we been the generation that failed? That's the fear I carry with me from this question. I wonder if my efforts have done anything much towards building the kingdom of God. I've run round a lot and used up a lot of energy, but has that achieved anything of lasting value? Being busy should never be confused with being effective. Did I commit myself to the most important concerns? Was I wise in discerning the signs of the times and the places to try and make a difference? Was I asleep to the really important issues? Perhaps you sometimes feel the same.

I've suggested that the three disciples Jesus took with him in Gethsemane were Peter the *warrior*, ready to jump in at any time to solve problems; John the *thinker*, whose special closeness to Jesus led him to ponder for the rest of his life what those three years really meant; and James the *follower*, who wanted to emulate Jesus in his approach to life and all that it threw at him. They fell asleep on the job, and we, too, might fall asleep in each of those areas of discipleship.

Warriors

There's a real possibility that we'll end up sleepwalking into immense danger through the rest of this century. Why has it taken a nona-genarian (David Attenborough) and a teenager (Greta Thunberg) to wake us up to the coming catastrophe of global warming and climate change? Why, even then, are we still so lacklustre in our response?

Actually, the answer is clear: it's the global diseases of self-interest, greed and short-termism that cause our social and political amnesia. Christians, though, ought to be shouting the loudest when humanity is on a path to self-destruction. God's world and its people are infinitely precious, and we're sleepwalking into the fire.

Teenagers, and even primary school children, have been on climate strikes worldwide, trying to tell their supposedly wiser parents and grandparents that they want to have a future. 'There's no plan B for the planet,' they've been saying. This is surely the place for Christians to be warriors, forgetting the small change of ecclesiastical politics and dealing instead in high-value currency, the survival of untold millions, if not the survival of humanity. If you really want to scare yourself, read *The Uninhabitable Earth* by David Wallace-Wells.[31]

Oxford philosopher Toby Ord in his book *The Precipice*[32] says that the likelihood of extinction before the end of the century has increased from 1 in 100 in the twentieth century (asteroid impact, stellar explosion, super-volcanic eruption) to 1 in 6 in the twenty-first century, with pandemics, nuclear war, climate change and 'unaligned artificial intelligence' (AI that doesn't share human values) heading the wolf-pack. 'The human-caused risks of the present are legion, and likely,' he writes.

The issues facing us are so numerous and so daunting that we're easily tempted to try and sleep through it all, muttering darkly those well-used words: 'It'll see me out.' But that's precisely what

William Wilberforce didn't do with slavery or Elizabeth Fry with women prisoners or Lord Shaftesbury with child factory workers or Peter Benenson with political prisoners or Chad Varah with people tempted to take their own lives or Martin Luther King with civil rights or Desmond Tutu with apartheid. The list of Christian warriors goes on. They didn't stay asleep.

We may not be warriors on their scale, but we can prayerfully determine what issues God is laying on our hearts and make a commitment to tackle those parts of the fire-storm. Being asleep isn't an excuse.

Thinkers

We may have been asleep in our *thinking* about what faith really means in a dangerous and complex world. Both Church and society need Christians with the ability and commitment to think deeply about faith and its implications for human flourishing. We need a grown-up faith for a world where religion plays a formidable role in the lives of at least 75 per cent of the global population, but where religion can also infantilize people and become dangerous.

Does the Church have the desire and the resources to do the hard thinking that society needs of us? William Temple's work made a major contribution to the thinking behind the Welfare State and David Sheppard's work on *Faith in the City* made government and nation take note of the plight of urban conurbations. The Church today needs to bring about a similar level of engagement with the major challenges society faces, not be enveloped by second-order issues.

Moreover, many of us might be asleep, or at least dozy, in our thinking through the nature of our beliefs. I once tried to interest Christians across many congregations in reading a minimum of three Christian books a year, to deepen understanding and appreciation of the faith. There was a minimal response.

A grown-up faith doesn't read the Bible as a manual with a coded message about the end of the world and when to hide under the table. A grown-up faith doesn't hold God responsible for every bad thing that happens to us and wonder what we've done to deserve it. A grown-up faith doesn't give up praying when things don't immediately go our way. A grown-up faith grows.

When Christians do a bit of reading or studying together, the results are almost always deeply enriching. It isn't a question of high intellectual firepower; it's just a question of thinking . . . and being awake.

Followers

At various times in my life I've got stuck as a follower of Jesus. I've had the textbook and seen the questions, but I haven't known the answers. I've known what my prayer life should be like, but it hasn't been like that at all. I've known the promise of growing in the likeness of Christ, but I've been forever slipping over on the ice. There was one long period when I reached out for the touch of God but always seemed to be clutching the air. I went to my spiritual director; I went on retreat; I prayed on, but there seemed to be no one pulling the other end of the rope that I was tugging so desperately. I continued with the conventions of religious practice but the reality had drained through the sieve.

It's possible to spend a lot of our Christian lives spiritually asleep. We may be comfortable on the dry riverbank of conventional religion, but the reality is that we're sleeping in the sun beside the remains of the picnic – a picnic that once seemed so satisfying. What I found in my own search was that I needed to wake up, wade into the water and start swimming properly. For me, that involved an encounter with God beyond the tyranny of words. It meant switching my spirit from transmit to receive, giving God space to be God *in* me and *for* me. It meant listening. It meant exploring silence, symbol, sacrament and story. It meant trying more spacious rhythms of prayer from Taizé and the Celtic tradition. It meant letting God be the 'God beyond God', not my own self-built idol.

It was simply one follower's way of getting closer to Jesus. Each of us has our own route. It could involve more extrovert prayer, prayer through nature, prayer while running, prayer through music, prayer in the shower, prayer with icons, prayer through choral evensong. The route doesn't matter; the reality does. The reality that comes from waking up.

'Are you asleep?' Jesus asks us. 'Quite possibly,' is the answer.

To ponder

- Do you think that you or your church have been asleep to the global threats to the sustainability of God's world?
- Do you think that you or your church have been asleep to the bigger issues of faith and the issues that really matter to people?
- Do you think that you or your church have been asleep to the need for mature Christians to go deeper in their spiritual exploration?

Prayer

A is for intercession; B is more contemplative.

A Pray for greater urgency and larger vision in our political systems as we face huge global challenges from climate change, nuclear instability, pandemics and various forms of terrorism. Pray for prophets and visionaries and people of peace.

B Recall your feelings and responses through the events of the last day. Then look ahead at what the next day or week holds. Now resolve to let the past go and not anticipate the future, but simply to live in the present moment – which, in fact, is the only moment in which your life is happening. It's now. Rest in the present, and in the presence of God.

16

'My God, my God, why have you forsaken me?'
Mark 15.34 (25–41)

My name is John, and I'm watching my best friend die. My name is John. My name is John . . . I have to hang on to whatever scraps of normality I can find, because the reality in front of me is unbearable. I can't let myself feel what he's feeling.

I say some psalms over and over in my head – psalms of despair and hope, disaster and triumph. I've always done this when I've been most afraid. It calms me, usually, but nothing can calm me now.

I look across at his mother, collapsed in a heap on the ground, shocked, rigid, brittle with pain. I move over to her, touch her lightly on the shoulder. She gives a sudden start, clearly brought back from a distant place where none of us would dare go. We hold hands. I can feel her body shaking.

I've begged her to leave or at least to sit a distance away from the horrific suffering of her son, but she's stronger than I am, and I think she's partly here for me too. We've had a deep bond since my mother died.

But how can this be happening? Less than a week ago, the welcome, the cheering, the palms, the city opening its arms to us. We were elated. It was what we'd wanted, prayed for; Zion welcoming its king. I can remember beaming all the way down the Mount of Olives, occasionally catching his eye with a broad smile. 'See, it's all coming true!' Perhaps I should have looked deeper and registered the sadness behind his eyes, even though those eyes still managed to smile at our innocence.

But now, just a few days on . . . What madness is this?

Jesus arrested in the night, a rigged trial, flogged to within an inch of his life, carrying the instrument of his own death through the streets. Then – I can't bear it – he's being laid on the ground, naked, and now being hammered, literally hammered, on to a cross.

With each blow of the hammer, his body flinches and his face screws up in unimaginable agony.

And he doesn't say a word.

Those soldiers know what they're doing. They're trained killers after all. A few swift blows and it's done. 'Just a job. Just another jumped-up messiah to dispose of. Hope he doesn't hang around too long in this heat. Nice tunic – his mother probably made it for him. We'll cast lots for it while we wait.'

Then that hideous cross is hauled up, the stuff of nightmares. It thuds into place, and Jesus is displayed before us in a way that we never dreamed possible. My friend – my generous, kind, wise, strong friend – reduced to an abject, naked criminal hanging from a tree.

All we can do is watch – his mother, a few other women, me and, of course, the awful members of the crowd who always gather to watch the pathetic victims of Roman justice. They just want to see how long it'll be before these poor wretches stop moaning and cursing and shaking their heads to get rid of the birds picking at their eyes.

He hangs there now, a tragic parody of a man, so diminished from the glorious figure we've been following around the hills and shores of Galilee. We revelled in the crowds, the healings, the excitement when he was going to preach; we loved listening to those golden words about the kingdom, about justice and love.

So diminished.

Yet I can't take my eyes off him. I'm appalled, but mesmerized. ('Yea, though I walk through the valley of the shadow of death, I will fear no evil.')

He pulls himself up on the nails that gouge through his wrists, just to grab another breath before slumping down again in pain that shoots through him. ('For you are with me; your rod and your staff, they comfort me.')

The simple truth is that he's suffocating. Soon he won't have the strength to pull himself up at all. ('You prepare a table before me, in the presence of my enemies; you anoint my head with oil; my cup overflows.')

Every so often he makes a supreme effort and manages to say something. He asks for a drink – and, despicably, he's given vinegar. ('Surely goodness and mercy shall follow me all the days of my life.')

He speaks with the two thieves alongside him and, if I've heard it right, he's promising one of them a reunion in heaven. ('And I shall dwell in the house of the Lord for ever.')

Have I heard this correctly – I need to check this with brave young Mary from Magdala – he's actually asking his Father to forgive his killers? It's beyond belief. (I start again: 'The Lord is my shepherd; I shall not want.')

The minutes are passing like hours. The sun is high, but it's getting strangely dark. I hear quiet sobbing nearby.

Now, just when I think that there'll be nothing else to come from him, there's another sentence – a question this time, almost whispered to himself, his eyes clouded and dark: 'My God, my God, why have you forsaken me?'

This time my blood turns cold. His relationship with his Father is so intimate, so intense, so much the core of all that he is, I can't even begin to conceive of that relationship breaking down. But that seems to be what he's going through – he's feeling rejected by the God who is everything to him.

Something within me dies.

• • •

'My God, my God, why have you forsaken me?' Has that ever been your question? No one could blame you if it had – Jesus certainly wouldn't.

The question is, perhaps, more important than the answer. Had God deserted Jesus? No, but is that what Jesus experienced at the time? Yes, certainly. It could hardly have been otherwise. When your whole body is consumed with unbearable pain, your vision is descending into darkness and the last scraps of your energy taken up with bare survival, you're not likely to be aware of anything except your life being chipped – or hacked – to pieces. It isn't a time for heavenly choirs.

That was Jesus' terrible human experience. On the cross, he so identified with the alienation of humankind that he lost contact with his heavenly Father. He inhabited the dilemma of being human so completely that he experienced the abandonment of God. He looked into the heart of darkness and held the burning world to himself in order to draw the sting, to disarm the dark powers. He absorbed the hatred, brutality, greed, selfishness, all that the world could throw at him – and resisted none of it. He simply took it. The pain and futility of the world funnelled down on to Jesus, and he met it with the only thing he had left: love.

Have you felt forsaken by God?

There's a statue of God in Chartres Cathedral. It's a beautiful piece, representing God on the seventh day of creation. If you pause to look carefully, you'll see a single tear rolling down God's face.

The pain of this world sometimes seems overwhelming. The average news bulletin is a catalogue of woes – a crisis is always blowing up somewhere, a disease is taking hold, a warlord is wreaking havoc, a famine is entering a critical phase, floods have destroyed an entire region, a 'lone wolf' has gone on the rampage at a school. When you turn to your own family and friends and count up the difficulties and sorrows that they're facing (and maybe *you're* facing), it's easy to forget the ordinary, happy days most people have had and the millions of acts of kindness given and received.

So where is God in this mad, messy world? The Christian answer is clear: on the cross. God enters the depth of human suffering in the person of Jesus. He knows it from the inside, identifying with the losses and tragedies that devastate the lives of men and women the world over. Many of us know all too well what those losses are. God in Christ, God in us, knows and shares what we go through.

This is no absentee father who sends his children money on their birthdays but can't be bothered to come and see them himself. God is here, and stays, and suffers with us. When our lives feel so damaged that we can hardly face the day, God has been there, in the person of his Son. What's more, God has gone to the edge, to breaking point. Except, God's love didn't break; that was the victory of the cross – ultimately, Love couldn't be broken.

Sometimes, perhaps, we might touch the edge of the experience of forsakenness that Jesus experienced. You never know when it might strike. I was once looking through a history magazine and came across a double-page photo of a family standing on a busy pavement during the Great Depression, with people walking by ignoring them. The father was holding a notice saying, 'Two parents, five children, thrown out on the street. Can anyone help?' The children all looked to be under six and it was the bewildered look on their little faces that undid me. They stood there helplessly, not knowing what was going on. Their vulnerability and innocence broke my heart. Somehow, at that moment, they represented the innocent suffering of the whole world and something came apart inside me. I touched the faintest edge of God's pain and what Jesus was soaking up on the cross. 'My God, my God, why have you forsaken me?'

In an olive grove the previous evening, Jesus had already asked if he could be spared this terrible path, but came to see that it was inevitable if he was to see through his proclamation of an alternative kingdom. He didn't need to ask why this was happening to him. He knew why; it's what the world does to goodness.

In our distress, facing disaster and with God off the radar, we often resort to that understandable question, 'Why me?' The answer given by someone who had MS was simple:

Why not? If I could make a cosmic deal, who would I put in my place? Who or what in my life would I give up in exchange for sound limbs and a thrilling rush of energy? No one. Nothing. I might as well do the job myself, now that I'm getting the hang of it.

There really is no escape from the sheer obtuseness of suffering as a fact of life. Julian of Norwich, the fourteenth-century mystic, wrote:

> If there is anywhere on earth where a lover of God is always kept safe, I know nothing of it, for it was not shown to me. But this was shown: that in falling and rising again we are always kept in that same precious love.[33]

It was the same precious love that held Jesus, even when he couldn't sense it. Jesus was, in fact, quoting from Psalm 22. He knew the Psalms, his prayer book, and, *in extremis*, the words were there, waiting for him. Moreover, Psalm 22 moves from this cry of despair to ultimate confidence in God: 'For he did not despise or abhor the affliction of the afflicted; he did not hide his face from me, but heard when I cried to him' (v. 24). Even in desperation and protest, Jesus knew to keep in touch with his heavenly Father, his only hope.

Perhaps this is the final answer to Jesus' terrible question. Faced with finality, where else can we turn? Abraham Lincoln lost two sons, and his wife suffered from mental illness. He knew tragedy. Finally, when he saw the graves of thousands of Union soldiers he wrote, 'I then and there consecrated myself to Christ.' When we are empty, when we have nothing, we might finally turn to the One who shared our nothingness, yet *is* everything.

But why would we offer our lives to a God who goes and gets himself killed? Perhaps the answer is: because he's the kind of God who can say to his Father, 'My God, my God, why have you forsaken me?'

Only a suffering God can help.

To ponder

- Have you ever felt forsaken or deserted by people you thought would stick by you?

- Have you ever felt forsaken by God? What happened next?
- Have you ever found that the 'suffering God' did help?
- Have you found the Psalms helpful in difficult times?

Prayer

A is for intercession; B is more contemplative.

A   Pray for the millions of Christians around the world who constantly live under persecution and threat. Pray for the work of Open Doors (<www.opendoorsuk.org>) and for international pressure to be brought to bear on the scandal and tragedy of human rights abuse.

A2 Use a large map of the world and place tealights on countries with the most oppressive regimes, lighting those candles as you pray for the victims.

B   Hold a hand cross and let your thoughts and prayers revolve around it, receiving anything that comes to mind and heart. Hold on to the cross for a time and maybe carry it with you for the rest of the day.

17

'Why are you weeping? Who are you looking for?'
John 20.15 (1–18)

I'm in a daze; it's all happened so fast. I knew it was dangerous, but three days ago, I thought that we were winning. The crowds loved him. They'd never heard anything like it. The word on the street was so positive.

But then, in a day – less than a day – it all collapsed and I'm in pieces.

But I had to come back.

I've lost him. I know I should say *we've* lost him, but it feels more personal than that. This was the man who gave me my life back. He poured light into every part of me and gave me a reason to live.

It's true that he stirred lots of confusing feelings in me as well. Was I attracted to him? Certainly. Was I in awe of him? Absolutely. Did he scare me sometimes?

Probably. There were times when it was hard to handle these conflicting emotions, but I knew that we had more important things to do than sort out my personal hang-ups.

And now he's gone. They scraped him down from that terrible cross only a day-and-a-half ago. His mother wanted to embrace him one last time and they laid him gently, ever so gently, over her knees. She was beside herself, broken beyond belief. We had to hold ourselves together for her sake, but I've never felt anyone's pain like that. The sight of mother and son – it was devastating.

I need a last moment to be near him. Not to do anything – what can I do? I just need to be near. So I'm on the path that he was carried along just two days ago. We were shocked beyond feeling. His body was heavy and awkward in death. The men carrying him nearly dropped him. I remember the ugly red stains on the linen shrouds.

We arrived at the gaping tomb waiting to swallow him up, and I remember the horrifying finality as the stone was rolled across the entrance. We thanked Joseph, the good man from Arimathea who had given his tomb to Jesus.

Then we left – all of us, lonely figures, feeling so empty. The next day was long and painful, nursing the wreckage of our hopes. Then we slept, exhausted. A second hopeless night.

Now dawn is creeping across the sky again and the birds are starting to sing their absurd songs of welcome to a new day. Why aren't they singing sad songs, muffled and full of tears?

I come round the final corner, forlorn and lonely, knowing what to expect, but I'm confused. This is the place, isn't it? So why is the stone not covering the entrance to the tomb? I look round. Is my memory playing tricks? No, this is it.

I creep up to the tomb, unsure now what I'll find. My mind is whirling, panicking. Grave robbers? Romans? Caiaphas? Who could have done this?

I'm not staying here any longer. I must get back to tell Peter and John. I turn and race back, thinking a thousand thoughts and none. Indistinct figures pass in the dawn light. I hammer on the door, gasping for breath, bits of sentences struggling out into the chill morning air. 'The Lord . . . not there . . . taken away!'

Immediately they fly out of the house, leaving me trailing behind and suddenly exhausted. I go back the way I came, scared, angry, bewildered. When I get there, they're standing outside, puzzled and undecided. Apparently, they've both been in. John got there first (Peter's a bit out of shape). They tell me what they've seen – the burial cloths lying on a shelf but with no body inside. The head cloth wrapped up separately for some reason. No sign of Jesus.

Peter gabbles all this to me, filling me in, while John is pensive – he looks as if he's working something out. We exchange bewildered explanations for a while but, finally, they give up and say that they're going home. Do I want to come? I say no, I want to stay around a bit longer. I just want some space to have a good cry, to let it all out. It's too much. I lost him on the cross and now I've lost him again from the tomb. I can't take any more. I sit down and cry and cry.

Eventually, I pull myself together, enough at any rate to look into the tomb to see what Peter and John have seen. Today is such a total shock that I'm almost not surprised to find two people already there. Am I imagining them? At least they're real enough that I can hear them speaking to me. They ask me why I'm crying, so I blurt out my despairing story that they've taken away my best friend and I don't know where they've put him.

Then I sense someone behind me. I turn. Just another man, probably the gardener. Why is this quiet place suddenly getting so crowded?

He speaks, the gardener, and his voice is warm and comforting. He repeats the question the two other strangers have already asked. 'Why are you crying? Who are you looking for?'

I'm getting beyond despair. 'Sir,' I say (I can at least be respectful), 'if it's you who's taken away my friend, please tell me where you've taken him. I won't be any trouble. I just want to take him away.' Though how on earth I propose to do that I really don't know.

The gardener stands there for a moment, looking at me. Then he says in a voice that wraps around me like smooth silk, 'Mary!'

My head spins. My world lurches off balance. That voice!

'Rabbouni!' My teacher!

I'm overwhelmed by a torrent of emotion, drowning in joy, rescued, thrilled beyond measure. He's alive! Instinctively, I reach out to touch him, to take his hand, to be reconnected, but he moves away. 'No, Mary,' he says. 'I'm sorry. Things have to be different now, for all of us.'

I'm confused. What's wrong with touch? We've all been so close; hugging is part of our life together. Jesus sees that I look hurt.

'Why are you weeping? Who are you looking for?'

'We have a new task now,' he says, 'bigger and better than ever, but I have to return to my heavenly Father.'

Joy and loss struggle within me, but I trust him. I do. It'll all become clear.

At least I know what I have to do now. I have to go and find the others and tell them the best news they've ever heard.

• • •

'Why are you weeping?' Because we've lost him.

It's the cry of millions of bereaved families every year across the globe as they grieve the loss of a loved one. The heartbeat of the family has stopped. The dear face with the crinkly smile – disappeared. The flow of funny stories, the love that filled the house – all melted away. It's the day the music died. That's why we weep.

'Who are you looking for?' The one we can never have back.

This is the agonizing experience of every one of us at some time or other, yet to each person it's as unique as if death has just been invented.

While I've been writing this book, my stepmother died. She was also my aunt and my godmother. (She married her brother-in-law, my father, long after their partners had died.) She lived fully, loved deeply and died gently. She was the last link with my much loved parents, whose long marriage gave me the stability, values and faith by which I live. She and my father had a final few years of mutual love and support before she was widowed a second time.

I try to imagine what kind of existence my stepmother and my parents might have now, after death, but I have to give up at first base. I'm out of my depth already. I dearly want them to be experiencing a new life in God, with all the 'radiancy of glory' and 'bliss beyond compare' that come as standard in 'that dear land of rest', but you can see how I'm already having to resort to the words of hymns to both *own* these concepts of life after death and also keep my distance from them. The truth is that I desperately want this new life for them but, equally, I don't want to fall into wishful thinking. I need to know that what I so much want to be the case isn't just the product of deep love, a rich imagination and an inability to face up to the harshness of an unfeeling universe. What can I stand on with reasonable confidence when contemplating life after death? On what can I base my hope?

I look towards three key beliefs: the nature of God, the teaching of Jesus and the astonishing event of the resurrection. First, the consistent witness of the Bible is that God is both loving and just, and although so much in life seems to contradict this conviction, the New Testament says that God will, in the end, put right all that's been hurtful and wrong in our experience. Justice and joy will be established at the heart of a new creation. Heaven and earth will be brought into full and final harmony because, ultimately, injustice can't coexist with a just God and, in the end, evil can't survive an encounter with Love.

What we blithely but properly call 'God's will' will, in fact, be done. The love of which justice is the social expression is the love from which St Paul says nothing can separate us: 'neither death, nor life, nor angels, nor rulers . . . nor height, nor depth, nor anything else in all creation' (Romans 8.38–39). Faith finds it impossible to believe that this love would end with death; that God would, at the end of our lives, simply throw away this precious part of his creation – us – as if we were so much cosmic waste. God could never just press 'delete' at the point of death. I believe that the nature of God as loving and just points to a future life beyond death.

Second, the reality of life after death is what Jesus believed and taught during his ministry. One of his most frequently used images was that of a banquet at the end of time, where all sorts of expectations would be turned upside down. The usual suspects would stay away or be displaced, and outsiders would find themselves invited to the top table. The seating arrangements might be different but one thing was certain: the banquet was definitely going ahead.

Now, if Jesus was so right about everything else he taught, why would he get this so wrong? He was clearly confident in the reality of our future life in God.

The clinching third argument comes in the resurrection of Jesus Christ from the dead. Without belief in the resurrection, the

Christian faith collapses, but with that belief *everything else* collapses if it stands in the way of a new creation.

In the New Testament, the resurrection is a pledge and promise of our own re-creation as part of the renewal of the whole cosmos:

> Now if Christ is proclaimed as raised from the dead, how can some of you say there is no resurrection of the dead? If there is no resurrection of the dead, then Christ has not been raised; and if Christ has not been raised, then our proclamation has been in vain and your faith has been in vain.
> (1 Corinthians 15.12–13)

Our future is inextricably linked to the future that Christ entered into after he had defeated death on the cross. You can't untangle the two; nor can you untangle the resurrection of Christ from the entire fabric of the Christian faith. The resurrection of Jesus is the central scandal of Christianity, and its greatest glory.

If there are grounds for believing in the reality of life after death, it's then natural to wonder in what way our loved ones could be alive – and whether or not we'll meet them again.

There's an obvious solace to be found in popular sentimental beliefs when we're looking into a dark future. Many bereaved people speak easily of their hope that their loved one is 'looking down' on them. Children are still reassured that Granny has gone 'to be with Jesus.' When Dick Sheppard, a well-known vicar of St Martin-in-the-Fields, died suddenly, one of the daily newspapers printed a large photo of his pulpit, empty except for an open Bible with a shaft of light striking across it. The caption said, 'Here endeth the first lesson.' Clearly a second lesson was anticipated.

However, such romantic images are less helpful when the culmination of life is seen as little more than our present existence with the bumps smoothed out or an afternoon tea with Aunty on cloud nine. There must be more to it than that, something more like the words of Prince Eugene Trubetskoy, who managed to exclaim as he was dying, 'The royal doors are opening! The great Liturgy is about to begin.'

'Why are you weeping? Who are you looking for?'

But, we might ask, in what way could that happen?

Inevitably, we resort to images. John V. Taylor, a former Bishop of Winchester, used the picture of our lives in the present being like those of children developing 'in the womb of the life to come', growing steadily but still not ready for birth. We're secure in the warmth and darkness of a little world that nourishes us and gives us contentment. We grow lungs without breathing, eyes without seeing, legs without walking. We stretch out our arms and think that we have freedom of movement. He built on the image further, saying:

> When the hour of our birth comes we will call it dying because it will be the end of the life we know and we shall be harshly sent out into the unknown. The fact that we cannot imagine heaven doesn't mean it isn't there, and rather than trying to understand it in advance, we had better get on with the life that is ours now, while our equipment for heaven grows unseen.[34]

Philosopher Helen Oppenheimer had another image:

> People have the kind of fragility and durability of [computer] software. The Creator, who values each person, has saved the data and will re-establish the pattern – maybe after a lapse of time – on different hardware.[35]

She goes on to say that it's fitting to be 'hopefully agnostic' about what heaven will be like:

> There's nothing wrong with enlivening one's imagination with a variety of pictures, all the better when they are evidently naive and creatively fanciful rather than deceptively literal.[36]

We can't be anything but naive when trying, from 'within the womb', to describe what real life after death will be like. Being too literal risks absurdity and it's liberating to be encouraged to be 'creatively fanciful'. We have no idea what it will be like, obviously, but when we do experience it we'll probably just say, 'Of course!' When the time comes, perhaps we might simply and joyfully let go of life and set off into God's good future.

'Why are you weeping?'

Because we haven't experienced it yet.

To ponder

- I wonder what 'the other disciple' actually believed when he went in and 'saw and believed'? The verse goes on to say that 'as yet they did not understand the scriptures that he must rise from the dead', so what did he believe at that stage?
- I wonder why, after such an experience, Peter and John just 'returned to their homes'?
- How confident are you that there is life after death, and why?
- What words would you use to make sense of the afterlife, to both yourself and to others?

Prayer

A is for intercession; B is more contemplative.

A Pray for people who have been recently bereaved and are now weeping for their loss. Remember also with gratitude those you have lost yourself, but who gave you much and helped to shape your life.

B In your prayerful imagination, go to the empty tomb with any people you know who have been bereaved or suffered another kind of loss. Imagine them meeting Christ at the tomb, then leave them there, trusting them to his care.

18

'Have you believed because you have seen me?'
John 20.29 (19–29)

The problem is, I wasn't there the first time. Sometimes I just needed to get away. I get on really well with the others but, from time to time, I need my own space. We'd been shut up in that same room for hours and, as dusk fell, I slipped out for some fresh air. I was careful not to draw attention to myself of course – everywhere felt dangerous.

So I missed him.

It didn't make it easier that they went on and on about it, telling one another what they'd seen. Even though they'd all seen the same thing, they had to keep talking about it. They said that Jesus had, somehow, simply appeared among them, greeted them and shown them his wounds. It really was him – they said! Then they looked round and realized that he wasn't there any more.

I mean, it just sounds so crazy, doesn't it? We know he was murdered on that hill. Those soldiers knew what they were doing. We know that he was buried, because Joseph, the council member from Arimathea, had given us his new grave, and some of us took the body there. We know that he was dead: a death is a death; you can't fake it. He'd stopped breathing. His blood had stopped flowing. His body had gone rigid. He was as white as marble. What more do you want?

So I've told them, unless I see for myself, unless I touch his hands where those nails went in, and his side where the spear was thrust to make sure he was dead, unless I get proof, I'm not going to believe it. I hate talking like this, but I'm so mixed up, I can't help myself.

The thing is, I really, really don't want to be taken in. I've got too much riding on this. If it's true . . . if it's really true . . . well, I'd happily die on the spot.

Days have passed and nothing else has happened. They're getting quieter about it, a bit less sure of themselves. They start telling each other the story again, then they fade away. I'm beginning to feel a bit more reassured about my doubts. It's not that I want to be right . . . I'd give anything – my life, as I said – for it to be true, but why drop in for half an hour, get everybody madly excited, then disappear again for a week without another word? It's all so far-fetched.

That said, I can't shake off the question – what was it that they experienced last week? My friends and I may be a little naive at times, but surely we're not that gullible?

So here we are. The truth is, we don't know what to do. We're waiting, but we don't know what we're actually waiting for. Peter has even been talking about going back home to Galilee and seeing what's happening there. He was one of the keenest to tell me about the tomb being empty and seeing Jesus last week.

I'm sitting in a corner, whittling a stick to make a toy for my kid brother. Some of them are chatting quietly. Andrew's eating some bread and humous. John's just sitting there, looking into the middle distance. One or two are sleeping – we do a lot of that.

Then I look up because something in the room has changed. The atmosphere is alive in some way. It's humming. It's – I don't know . . .

Yes, I do. He's here!

Shock. Stillness. A smile.

'Peace be with you.'

Those words; that voice. It's as if he not only says the words but he actually hands peace over to us as a tangible gift. Peace. It's a mix of 'no need to be scared', 'isn't it good to be together?' and 'bless you' all in one.

He looks around the room at us until his gaze settles on me. I don't know what to do or what to say. I don't even know who I am! I shut my mouth, which I find has somehow fallen open. I shrink into myself, but I'm also drawn towards him. He always had that power of attraction. Now he seems positively compelling. But gentle with it.

How is he doing this?

He's speaking to me. It's as if everyone else has faded away. It's just the two of us. And he's speaking straight into my heart.

'Thomas. You want proof. Here, touch my hands.' He holds them out. Offers me his wounds. 'Or my side – here,' he says, indicating where he must surely still be in pain from that spear wound. Surely . . . but is he?

I feel something dissolve inside me. I have no resistance left. I'm overwhelmed by a flood of emotions – utter amazement, pure happiness, sweet surrender.

I find myself on the floor. I want to bow down, forehead on the floor, but I also want to look into his eyes. I want to understand, and then find I don't even want to think. I want to laugh, but find that I'm weeping instead. The one thing I don't want to do is demean his generosity by touching his wounds. He's come to meet me, all the way from wherever miracles come from. I accept. I accept.

'My Lord and my God!' It slips out unannounced. I can't say anything less.

Above me, a soft-spoken challenge: 'Have you believed because you've seen me?'

I'm so sorry. Honestly. I wanted so much to believe it was true. I needed proof.

'Blessed are those who haven't seen, but have still come to believe.'

Lord, I get it. We've had a privilege that others won't have, can't have. We've been so fortunate, so amazingly fortunate.

I scramble up from the floor. I look round.

But he's gone.

• • •

'Have you believed because you have seen me?'

Obviously, we won't hear that particular question being put to us, but we should hear the next bit: 'Blessed are those who have not seen and yet have come to believe' (v. 29).

That's us.

We truly are blessed if we've come to believe because, in today's world, that isn't straightforward. We live in a landscape of scepticism, if not hostility, and it takes courage to stay in lane as we travel the highway of faith.

Thomas has had to endure being known as the 'doubting' apostle for as long as people have read John's Gospel, but we do him a disservice. He wasn't so much an agonized doubter as a bereft and honest follower who simply didn't want to be taken in. He didn't want to be deluded by his dreams. On the other occasions we encounter him in the Gospels, he's either committing himself totally – 'Let us also go, that we may die with him' (John 11.16) – or he's asking Jesus to make things clearer, so that they can follow him – 'Lord, we do not know where you are going. How can we know the way?' (John 14.5).

Thomas had so much hanging on the truth that he'd found in Jesus, he couldn't bear to risk it crumbling into dust. He wanted to give everything for the truth, not for a lie. He was too honest for that. He had to know.

'Blessed are those who have not seen and yet have come to believe.' Us. You, me and millions of others. How, then, do people come to believe when they haven't seen?

It was just as crazy for the disciples but at least they had the evidence of their own eyes. In John's Gospel, the beloved disciple is convinced by the way that the cloths are arranged in the tomb; Mary is convinced when she hears her name; the disciples are convinced by Jesus appearing to them; Thomas could have been convinced by touching Jesus, although we're not told whether or not he did.

But what about us, 'who have not seen'? Not surprisingly, there's no single route map, just 'you are here' and a final satnav location. The routes between the two are many and various, personal and tailor-made. But let's look at some of the more familiar paths that people take, all the while remembering the words that philosopher Blaise Pascal attributed to God:

Console yourself; you would not seek me if you had not found me.[37]

Indeed, it seems to be the case that, in very many journeys to faith, there's some prior, unrecognized awareness of God, some divine discontent, that's already lurking within. Nothing that's been articulated, just a rumour, ready to be awakened.

When something breaks up the surface of atheism that's been hard-baked under the sceptical sun of our unbelieving culture, there's often a cautious green shoot of faith ready to emerge. That shoot of inconvenient truth gradually begins to take root and grow.

So what is it that breaks up the surface initially?

One thing is *nature* and nature's ordinary miracles. I've been brought to a standstill by natural wonders more often than by anything else. Most of us have marvelled at a scene that has been 'breathtaking', 'heartstopping', 'mindblowing'. Note the images in those words. We run out of road with our ordinary language. 'Wonderful' and 'marvellous' seem too timid, 'stunning' too overused, 'extraordinary' too ordinary.

Perhaps we're being taken beyond the thing-in-itself and attracted to the Maker of miracles, who gives us a million glimpses of heaven in the feast that nature puts before us. We know there's a dark story in nature, too, and that has to be taken with the utmost seriousness, but what we're looking at here is the common recognition of 'something more', the 'remainder' that eludes all attempts to wish it away.

Another experience that breaks up the hard-baked surface of unbelief is *beauty*, often experienced through the arts. Johann Wolfgang von Goethe said that we should:

hear a little music, read a little poetry and see a fine picture every day in order that worldly cares may not obliterate the sense of the beautiful which God has implanted in the human soul.

134

But what is beauty? We can't weigh or measure it or even properly explain it. In one sense it's a personal preference but, in another, it makes a claim on us which seems more objective than that. Albert Camus saw that:

> Beauty is unbearable, drives us to despair, offering us a glimpse of an eternity that we should like to stretch out over the whole of time.

We may find that we've been ambushed by beauty.

Beauty implants in our souls a glimpse of eternity. This is the green shoot that many later recognize was already there before they made any conscious entry into a living tradition of faith.

Beauty is unsettling. It awakens something in us that won't go to sleep. This glimpse of beauty may be in a person, the joy of a child's shy smile, a kitten turning somersaults with a toy, a glorious painting or piece of music. For writer Francis Spufford, it was the poignant beauty of the slow movement of Mozart's clarinet concerto, heard in a café one far remembered morning; music, he said, that sounded like mercy.[38]

There are also *special people* who can sometimes be the catalyst for faith. *New York Times* columnist David Brooks grew up with conventional secular assumptions but, as he experienced more of life and met more and more interesting people, he wrote this:

> It didn't make sense to me that they were just sacks of genetic material. It only made sense to me that they had souls. That there was some piece of them that had no material dimension, no size or shape, but gave them infinite dignity, every single one of them.[39]

Brooks glimpsed 'another layer of life' and eventually came to faith. Many of us also could name the special people who showed us something deeper and different.

What else might lead people to belief? *Shock.* We all have to face tragic disruption of our lives at some point. If nothing else, bereavement does it. So does divorce, serious illness, betrayal and myriad other experiences in which life is unceremoniously turned upside down. W. H. Auden was sitting in a cinema in Manhattan, watching the news of the horrors that the Nazis had perpetrated on the Jews, and suddenly his optimistic view of the world was confronted by the reality of evil:

> If I was to say *that* was evil, I had to have a standard by which to do so. I didn't have one. I needed to be able to say that this was wrong.[40]

That experience unblocked his resistance and he found his way to faith.

American writer Barbara Ehrenreich, famous for her atheistic rationalism, turned out to have had a mystical experience in her adolescence so strange that she didn't even dare speak or write about it for decades – but it haunted her. Eventually, in later life, she found that she had to:

> condense all the chaos and mystery of the world into a palpable Other . . . because ultimately we may have no choice in this matter . . . it may be seeking us out.[41]

In this way, shock can loosen our secular convictions.

Interestingly, a gentler encounter with *inwardness* can have the same effect. In a world pounded by noise and forever chasing its tail, the experience of stillness, silence and space can be revelatory. The popularity of retreats and pilgrimages, mindfulness and 'time out', meditation and spiritual direction demonstrates that something shifts inside us when given the opportunity and space to do so. The experience allows us to take down our walls and renegotiate our boundaries. We take the lids off the sealed boxes of ideas and beliefs that we've accumulated about life and take another look inside. If we neglect inwardness in favour of noise and constant action, we might miss the opportunity of a lifetime.

Nature, beauty, special people, shock, inwardness – these are just examples of the kinds of experiences that might enable the shy green shoots of faith to break up the surface of unbelief that lie over many lives today.

We may seem to have travelled far from Thomas, whose desire for integrity in his own belief set him looking for 'proof'. He found, instead, that his needs were met by an encounter with Christ that utterly relativized his limited ambition. He shot straight from ground level to mountaintop as he formulated the ultimate words of faith: 'My Lord and my God.' He was the first person in the Gospels to recognize that in Jesus they had not only found the Messiah (who in popular belief at the time was more human than divine) but they had also found God.

'Blessed are those who have not seen and yet have come to believe.' It may not be easy, particularly for those brought up on a diet of relentless secularism, but there is one last piece of hidden evidence buried in the heart of our culture that continues to break up the surface of unbelief, and that's the quiet *presence of Christ*. The following words from Richard Harries sum up the situation for many of us very well:

> I am acutely aware of the case that can be made against what the Christian faith claims. Indeed the situation has been well likened to one in a good detective story. All the clues seem to point in a particular direction. But the good detective is struck by a small piece of evidence that suggests it is not quite so simple and that the truth lies elsewhere. The case against a wise and loving power behind the universe is massive and it is easy to sympathise with people like Stephen Fry who explode against the idea of God . . . But there is a piece of evidence [that was] almost totally overlooked by the world at the time, and largely hidden today, which suggests that the truth is stranger and more astonishing than that; and that is Jesus crucified and risen.[42]

I think Thomas would agree.

To ponder

- I wonder what the disciples thought was going on during the week between the two appearances of Jesus?
- Can you trace the origins of your belief? Do they echo any of the suggestions mentioned above: nature, beauty, special people, shock, inwardness, the presence of Christ?
- What do you think might be the most helpful points of connection for people starting on a journey of faith today?

Prayer

A is for intercession; B is more contemplative.

A Pray for anyone you know who you would love to find faith. Hold them before God and join your love to God's love for that person. Repeat regularly.

B 'My Lord and my God.' Live with that phrase for a while. Repeat it. Relish it. Let your mind wander into it, look around, then rest in it. Don't hurry out.

19

'What are you discussing with each other?'
Luke 24.17 (13–35)

This is the worst day. We've been following a dream and it's turned into a nightmare. We're trudging back to Emmaus with our dreams in tatters, which is what happens when the sky falls in.

Just a few days ago it was so different. Jesus was in sparkling form as he taught and chatted with us around the Temple. I know my wife Mary and I aren't (weren't . . .) among his closest friends, but we've been following him whenever we can. His words poured into our hearts like crystal-cold water in a heatwave. It was a waterfall of truth, and we soaked it up as if we'd never heard truth before.

So how has it all gone so catastrophically wrong? We've seen that same man hanging on a cross, enduring a torrent of hate from those smug, self-serving guardians of the law. I feel like joy itself died there – his joy in life and ours in him. It's no wonder Mary and I are sniping at each other, like husbands and wives sometimes do. We're crushed, all out of patience. We've no resistance left.

It takes a while before we realize that there's someone walking beside us. I glance up, no more than that. We don't know him. Another wanderer.

'What are you talking about?' he asks.

It's such a naive question, we stop in our tracks. Mary and I look at each other, united again. 'You mean you really don't know? Are you the only stranger in Jerusalem who hasn't heard what's been happening there these last few days?' It probably comes out sharper than it should have done.

'What things do you mean?'

My annoyance dies down. Perhaps I need to talk to a stranger to get some perspective on all that's happened.

We start walking again. I tell him about Jesus, how we've never met anyone like him, how his teaching tugged at our hearts, how he gave us glimpses of the real kingdom of God, so beautiful and so powerful. I tell him how our so-called leaders handed him over to the Romans, who promptly did that typical Roman thing and crucified him.

'But we had hoped . . .' I start to say, suddenly realizing just how pathetic it sounds. 'We had hoped that he would be the one to rescue us at last, to free us from Rome and our own hopeless leaders.' I glance at him again. He's still just listening, attentive. It helps.

I go on. 'And now, just to rub it in, we've got some crazy stories going around about some of the women in our group going to the tomb and finding it empty or something. It's just fantasy, pure fantasy.'

I find that we've stopped again. I've run out of emotion. I'm empty, exhausted. There's nothing more to say.

Silence. We had hoped . . .

I look up. He's smiling. 'I'm sorry,' he says, 'but I think you've got this wrong. Let me tell you the real story . . .' He takes the entire sweep of our Scriptures and tells it in a whole new way. He keeps pointing to all the references to the Messiah and showing that the Messiah was bound to suffer for the people. It wasn't so much that he was going to save us *from* suffering; rather, he was going to save us *through* suffering. It's a whole new way of looking at the Messiah, a whole new way of thinking about God.

All the time, I have a nagging feeling somewhere deep inside – a connection, an echo, a memory. I'm not sure what it is but, as I try to grab this whatever-it-is, it slips away . . .

'What are you discussing with each other?'

I realize, all of a sudden, that we're back in Emmaus. I've been so absorbed in what the stranger's been saying that I haven't noticed the path, and now the familiar scattering of houses. The stranger is going to take his leave and move on and, suddenly, I realize how much I want this conversation to continue.

'Please come in. Have something to eat with us. Our house is right here.' He comes in and sits down.

It's not a very special house but it's comfortable. We've been here . . . must be ten years. We have some food in the cupboard left over from last week, when we set off for Jerusalem feeling so excited. Bread (a bit hard), olives, cheese, fruit, a jug of wine – the usual. We settle down to eat.

Gradually, we fall silent. I don't know why. Something in the atmosphere is shifting. The stranger is doing something quite odd; he's beginning to take over my role as host of this meal. He's picking up the bread, saying a blessing over it, breaking it, offering it to us.

That's it! That's who! No, it can't be! This is crazy. What's happening here? I can't breathe. Could it be? I look round. Mary? Yes, she's still sitting at the table, in a kind of trance, but the stranger . . . The stranger's gone.

'M-Mary,' I stammer after a minute or two. 'How were you feeling when he was telling us that other story of the Scriptures – the one he called the real one? My whole heart rose up. I felt warm right through, as if I was recognizing the truth for the first time. It was like coming home when you've been homesick all your life. How about you?'

We're striding up and down the room now, beside ourselves with a fierce energy, unable to control our thoughts and feelings. Except for one thing. 'We must get back,' I cry, hoarse with joy and laughter. 'We must tell the others.'

We shoot out. I don't even know if we closed the door. We run, leap, whoop for joy. This is no time for walking. The same path, the one we laboured along so recently, laden with tattered memories. Now it's a path of gold. We don't notice the miles.

We burst into the house. Before we're able to say anything, a chorus of voices is telling us that Jesus really has risen, and actually appeared to Peter. 'Yes, yes,' we say, 'and listen to this . . .' We have to tell them about the beautiful stranger who turned out to be Jesus.

'How did you know it was him?' one of them asks.

'It was how he took the bread, blessed it, broke it and gave it to us,' I say. 'It was nothing special, but it was exactly like he always did it. We knew. We just knew. It was like my heart suddenly burst open and love poured in. Ask Mary, she'll tell you what happened.'

I look for Mary. She's sitting on the floor leaning against the wall, exhausted.

And smiling as if she's never smiled before.

• • •

Jesus asked Cleopas and Mary, 'What are you discussing with each other?' It was a perfectly reasonable question to ask in that context.

It's also a perfectly reasonable question to ask now, in a different context. What are *we* discussing with one another? What are our personal conversations about, and our national ones? What do people seem to be concerned about at present? It seems to me that our conversations, like that of Cleopas and Mary, are often problem-centred and we habitually slip into narratives of despair. We find ourselves complaining about people we know or politicians and public figures parading their prejudices on social media or simply 'the way the world is' (often compared with how it used to be).

Those two unhappy disciples had good reason to lament the collapse of their hopes. Their dreams had gone sour overnight. The same can happen to any of us in a world of chance and accident. One visit to a consultant, one letter in the post, one drink too many, one argument too visceral, one mistake on the road, one unexpected bill – small steps can lead any of us to the cliff edge.

At the global level, there's more than enough to feed the narrative of hopelessness. Climate change and the destruction of the planet, cyber threats that could destroy entire economies, diseases that run out of control, racism and the resurgence of the far right, nuclear and biological terrorism, a world bleeding with injustice and corruption . . . We face massive uncertainties so why should we not think that this is a sinking ship?

Cleopas and Mary (assuming that the second person could be Mary – see John 19.25) could only see a jigsaw of confused pieces. It made no sense that Jesus should die. For many, living in our gilded cages in the West, it makes no sense that behind the glittering shop window of a culture obsessed with sex, celebrity and money lies the threat of imminent collapse.

There's just one thing that subverts this dark narrative: the resurrection of Jesus Christ.

The resurrection is the great reversal that challenges our narrative of despair. It puts at the very heart of existence a trajectory of possibility instead of a trajectory of tragic inevitability. The simple word for this is hope.

Vaclav Havel, former President of the Czech Republic, wrote:

> Hope is a state of the mind, not a state of the world . . . It's a dimension of the soul; it's not essentially dependent on some particular observation of the world or estimate of the situation, it's an orientation of the spirit, an orientation of the heart. It transcends the world that's immediately experienced and it's anchored somewhere beyond its horizons . . . Hope isn't the conviction that things will work out well, but the certainty that something will make sense, regardless of how it turns out.[43]

For Christians, this conviction isn't based on conventional optimism naively whistling in the dark. It's based on an event that wrenched the wheel away from death and brought an entirely new dynamic into the heart of not just our thinking but also the very fabric of the world. The problem is that we've got so used to hearing and repeating the narrative of negativity that we find it hard to believe there's another way to tell the story.

For many years, I supported a football team that had discovered the trick of continuous failure. I won't name the team for fear of reprisals – football fans are fiercely loyal, no matter how abysmally their team performs. However, these same fans kept up a constant lament about the woefully bad players, the manager, the owner, the pitch, the club cat and anything else that could be blamed. But if you listened to the away fans visiting us and celebrating the game they'd just won, you would have heard an entirely different story. One game, two narratives. How you tell the story depends on your point of view and what energizes your spirit.

Christians are energized by the resurrection rather than the narrative of negativity. 'I want to know Christ and the power of his resurrection,' wrote Paul (Philippians 3.10). 'So if you have been raised with Christ, seek the things that are above' (Colossians 3.1). The resurrection transforms the way in which believers look at life. The old narrative has been changed irrevocably. As Havel said, 'Hope is a state of the mind, not a state of the world.'

However, we mustn't let this confidence become trite piety. The world is indeed in a dire state. Open any serious newspaper; watch any responsible newsfeed. Moreover, personal tragedy blights countless lives. Many individuals experience life as dark and threatening. Many an empty shell hides behind a smiley face. In life as we know it, both globally and personally, there's no safety mechanism.

However, God is hidden in the cracks of these situations. There's a distinctive Christian protest against all this pain, a protest powered by the energy of the resurrection. In looking for racial justice in society, Martin Luther King Jr said in a speech:

> I know you are asking today, 'How long will it take?' I say to you, however difficult the moment, however frustrating the hour, it will not be long, because truth pressed to the earth will rise again. How long? Not long, because no lie can live forever. How long? Not long, because you shall reap what you sow. How long? Not long, because the arc of the moral universe is long but it bends towards justice.[44]

The resurrection is the implacable protest of love and hope against despair.

Moreover, this narrative-changing experience of the resurrection is possible for individuals in the most appalling situations. I once went to a reception at the Houses of Parliament in Westminster and a North Korean widow was speaking of her experience as a Christian in a country with a fierce antipathy to faith. Her husband had been tortured and killed for sharing his faith. Her daughter had died of starvation during one of the periodic famines. The widow herself had been sent to a labour camp where the small number of Christians used to meet in the toilets as they were so unhygienic no one else would linger there. She told us how people died in the camp every day from hunger, illness and brutality; but, fundamentally, she said, they died because they had no hope. Christians in the camp had the hope of Jesus and the resurrection in their hearts, so they were much more likely to survive. They told a different story and were held by it. Resurrection hope saves lives.

When faced with the sorrow of this world, Christians are called to be apostles of resurrection, just like the first believers. The message that compelled them into action and which they carried to the far corners of the known world is that Christ is risen and so we are never alone, never separated from the love of God. This isn't a fluffy message, suggesting that we make a few changes to our comfortable lifestyles while still living with the unexamined priorities of a competitive, consumer culture. Rather, it's an explosive recipe for life that's been discovered by those who've been scorched by the love of God and are now living in the giddy fullness of the risen Christ. It means starting from a different place with a different Companion.

That's what Cleopas and Mary discovered on a day that started with a despondent trudge home to Emmaus and ended with a riotous reunion back in Jerusalem. Their narrative was fundamentally changed from one of despair to one of hope and possibility. We never hear of them again. We hear of the remaining 11 disciples, of course, and all but one of them died a violent death because they became apostles of the resurrection and wouldn't keep quiet. Their faith didn't protect them from harm, but it completely altered their perspective on what mattered. That perspective released them from fear and enabled them to set about radically changing society, a process that continues to this day.

'What are you discussing with each other?' sounded like an innocent question but, as with all of Jesus' questions, it needed a health warning. Nothing would ever be the same again.

To ponder

- What do you think might have happened afterwards to Cleopas and Mary, and other followers of Jesus who had walk-on parts in the Gospels?
- Are there areas of your life in which you have a habitual 'narrative of despair'? What could you do about that?
- In what areas of our national and global conversations do you think that we need to change the narratives? How could that happen?
- Could you point to areas of personal or national life in which the narrative did change, and say how that happened?

Prayer

A is for intercession; B is more contemplative.

A Pray for people on pilgrimage at present, on their way to Santiago de Compostela or Canterbury, Rome or the Holy Land; those making their way to Lourdes or Walsingham, Iona or Taizé, Lindisfarne or any of the hundreds of other holy places at home and abroad. Pray, too, for those whose responsibility it is to receive and encourage the pilgrims who arrive at holy places.

B Go on an 'Emmaus walk' yourself – a real walk or one in your imagination. Let Jesus come alongside you and tell him what you're thinking and feeling. Then let the conversation unfold.

20

'Simon son of John, do you love me?'
John 21.16 (15–22)

I knew it had to happen. The Conversation.

Seven of us had come back home from that traumatic time in Jerusalem. We'd waited around in Jerusalem long after the incredible weekend when it all happened, but we didn't know what to do there. Sometimes Jesus was with us, then he wasn't. Surely he'd tell us what to do, we thought, but he didn't. He left us high and dry. Coming back to Galilee seemed the obvious thing to do. Time with families, some quiet fishing, stuff we knew about.

What we hadn't reckoned on was Jesus appearing to us again, right on the shore, just like old times – though, of course, it was nothing like the same when you think of all we'd been through together. But there he was, guiding us to a huge catch of fish, smiling as we struggled to haul it in. I made a bit of a fool of myself when I jumped into the water to get to him. ('So what's new?' you're probably thinking!)

It was the charcoal fire that did it. Jesus was busy preparing breakfast for us – he'd got the bread, we'd got the fish – but that familiar smell took me back to another charcoal fire, a serving girl pointing in my direction, all eyes looking at me, a cock crowing, Jesus knowing what I'd done . . . I shivered at the memory I'd tried so hard to bury.

After breakfast, he suggests that we have a little walk, just him and me – or, rather (let's be honest), the risen Jesus with the so-called friend who failed him! I've been expecting this conversation to happen sometime. I take a deep breath. 'Yes, of course,' I answer, trying to sound calm. I'd be happy to talk about anything . . . apart from what I know is coming. How his mother is, for example, or how Dad's fishing business is doing this year or the state of the roads around Galilee or if he's got any plans for what to do next . . . (I'm obviously getting desperate here).

But I know what it has to be about. Fair enough. I completely lost my nerve in that courtyard. It was dark. I didn't know anybody there. Jesus had been arrested. My world had suddenly fallen apart. Then they accused me of – what? – being with Jesus? Was that it? And I couldn't handle even that, despite all those big promises I'd made earlier in the evening.

It was more than that, of course: I couldn't face the prospect of a cross. I just folded inside. I'm so sorry.

For a while, I'm lost in the memory of it all, thoughts too deep for tears . . .

We set off, walking in silence along the shore.

Then Jesus says, in a calm voice, 'Simon son of John, do you love me?'

The words cut right into me. What? What's he asking? Do I love him? Do I love him!

'Yes, Lord; you know that I love you.' Of course he knows. Why is he asking me this rather than why I was so rubbish that night, why I let him down so badly?

'Then be a shepherd and feed my sheep.'

I hear it, but I don't get it. I'm a fisherman, not a shepherd. How can I feed sheep? Which sheep anyway? Where's this conversation going? I look out over the lake, that beloved lake – scene of my innocence before all the excitement of going off with Jesus. It's safer to look out over the lake than to look at Jesus. I'm still too embarrassed by my failure.

He stops and turns towards me, looking me straight in the eye. He says again, 'Simon son of John, do you love me?'

The question hangs in the air. What's going on here? He's gone back to the way he first knew me, as Simon son of John, the fisherman. That was before he called me Peter, the rock. (Some rock!)

But I think I understand. He's giving me another chance. He's not going to humiliate me, make me grovel. He's inviting me to go back to the start and try again. 'Simon son of John.' So, yes, absolutely yes!

'Yes, Lord, you know that I love you!' I say it with even more conviction than last time. I feel something loosening, like an iron band that's been round my chest beginning to slacken off.

'Then do the right thing and look after my sheep.'

I'm getting it. He's meaning look after his followers. He's not going to be around for ever (we kind of realize that) and he wants me to take on the responsibility of keeping them safe. He's often pointed out how shepherds – good shepherds anyway – take really good care of their sheep, lying across the entrance to their folds at night, fighting off wolves that might come to attack them.

He's trusting me to do that for his friends and followers when he's gone. Me, of all people! It sounds crazy but then he always seems to know what people are really capable of, both good and bad, even more than they do themselves. He even told me that I would deny knowing him three times that very night. At the time, it seemed daft. Me, Peter, the rock man, letting him down? Never!

But I did.

He has this uncanny way of knowing what's in the heart of people he meets, so maybe he sees how deeply I regret what I did and how it's changed me. Maybe he sees that, actually, I could take on this role and be a shepherd. That would be amazing – if I could do it.

He puts a hand on my shoulder. Still that even gaze of his which sees right into you.

'Simon son of John, do you love me?'

If I'm honest, I find myself getting a bit annoyed this time. We've been over it already. He knows that I love him. He's told me what I should do, so why do we have to go over it all again? I try not to show my irritation, though I know I have no right to feel that.

But then I realize why he's asking me yet again. Of course. Three times I denied him; three times I have to stand up and be counted. So I try to hold his gaze and say, with even greater conviction, 'Lord, you know everything about me. You know that I love you.'

'Then this is the charge I'm giving you,' he says. 'Look after my followers, and build them up and care for them with your own life, because it'll come to that. Remember when you were a youngster here . . .' He looks around at the tranquil scene – water lapping the shore, birds in full voice, familiar hills in the hazy morning light. 'You were free to roam round Galilee, wherever you liked. But when you're much older, I'm afraid that other people will decide your future and they'll take you where you don't want to go.'

This is turning serious, but whatever that future event is, it's a long way off. I've just been given the most astonishing responsibility. I'm absolutely determined not to let Jesus down again. I'm not turning back this time.

'Peter,' he says, giving me back my name. 'Follow me.'

Just that.

I'm kind of stunned. The all-wrong, upside-down life I've felt I've been living since that terrible night has just been turned the right way up again, but with a health warning about the future. I'm in shock. I need the pressure off me for a while, the conversation to turn somewhere else. I'm vaguely conscious that John has been following us at a discreet distance.

'Lord, what about John?' I ask. 'What should he do?'

But, of course, I get the response I half expect already.

'Peter, that's between him and me. That's our business, not yours. Your job is to do what I asked: follow me.'

It's as clear a command as I've ever had. That's what's going to stay with me. Put one foot in front of the other. Don't even think about turning back. Follow him wherever it leads.

Because I love him.

• • •

It's one of the most personal questions that Jesus could ask us, but let's imagine it. 'Do you love me?' he asks. What will you say?

We were still in bed one morning when we heard one of our small daughters making her way upstairs. We could hear her practising her speech. 'Sorry, sorry, sorry, sorry, sorry, sorry . . .' She'd dropped a bottle that had smashed all over the kitchen floor and she knew she had to own up. It's surprising how many 'sorrys' you can say while climbing a flight of stairs. Bless her – it was an accident.

The lovely thing about the remarkable conversation between Jesus and Peter is that nowhere does Jesus seem interested in hearing Peter's abject apologies. There's no sense of Jesus looking down from a great height and saying to Peter that he might just be forgiven if he will grovel in front of him as the failure he is and be full of remorse. He's only interested in seeing if Peter is ready to be restored and given a new future. That's not to say Jesus ignored the problem. He went straight to the location of the pain and, like a skilled surgeon, applied the knife that healed.

In that one conversation Jesus did three things: he forgave the past, reinstated Peter to his role among the disciples, and invited him to share in Jesus' own ministry. He was to be the shepherd and overseer of the small group of followers ('my sheep') who would soon mushroom in number and set about changing the world. Peter would still sometimes get muddled (see his different responses in Acts to the inclusion of Gentiles in the early Church), but he would never turn back again. He would hold on, even when tempted to run away from his own crucifixion in Rome – if the 'Quo Vadis' tradition contains any truth.

Those three things – forgiveness, reinstatement, sharing Jesus' own ministry – were all achieved by that innocent question: 'Do you love me?' It's the question that he also asks us.

For both Peter and us the nub of the question is, 'Do you love me enough to accept your own vocation and ministry, and to follow me wherever that may lead?' The problem is that many of us don't seem to understand our Christian faith as giving us a ministry. 'Ministry', we think, is about being ordained or having some other authorized position in the Church. Well, no it's not, according to the New Testament.

All of us are called to offer ourselves in the service of Christ and his Church with whatever skills, experience and personal qualities we've gathered along the way.

The heart of the problem is that we tend to judge ourselves too harshly and minimize our gifts. I do it myself. Not long ago, I found myself writing in my spiritual journal, 'Have I done any good or have I talked endlessly about doing good without doing much of it myself? Have I just lived a privileged, white, middle-class Western life without significant challenge or difficulty and without putting even a brick or two into the foundations of the kingdom of God?' The next day, I received an email from a generous friend who wrote, 'For some reason I feel prompted to send this from my devotional reading today: "The criterion for discipleship is not a perfect past but a faithful heart, trusting for a glorious future, while prayerfully serving in an imperfect present."' I still don't know if I've done much good, but I do know that I've done my best (usually) and God values my faithful foolishness.

We're called to prayerful service, not to change the world by the weekend. None of us comes with a perfect CV, but if we answer Jesus' question, 'Do you love me?' by saying 'Yes, Lord, you know that I love you', then we are, inevitably, called to offer what we have. It may be just five loaves and two fishes, but remember what happened before through simple fare.

Another problem can be the temptation to compare ourselves to others. We easily slip into thinking that others are much better qualified to be doing something for Christ than we are. That may well be true, of course, but this sense of inferiority denies Christ and his Church so much loving service. It also denies us our opportunity to grow as Christian disciples, and it leaves us instead merely managing our reputation. (How am I doing? What do people think of me? Wouldn't so-and-so do it much better?) When Peter asked Jesus about John, who was following behind on the beach, Jesus said to Peter, 'What John does is between him and me. Your job is to do what I've asked you: follow me.' Don't compare your calling with that of others.

Peter followed all too faithfully. He followed Jesus to his own death, probably in Rome. The other disciples followed Jesus to their own deaths, too, in various parts of the world. And still it goes on. Once we answer Jesus' question with 'Yes, Lord, you know that I love you', it could lead anywhere. There's no turning back . . . or that's the theory. How would any of us in the West respond to the challenge facing 260 million Christians around the world who are living daily under persecution and oppression and, in some cases, the real threat of imprisonment and death? We just don't know. Context is everything.

As I was writing this, news came through that Kande Mudu, a 27-year-old Christian convert in a village called Bari in Jharkhand, north-east India, had been killed because of his loyalty to his faith. He had become a Christian four years before and his family were the only Christians in the village. A group of armed men arrived at the family home and demanded that Kande come outside. He told his wife that he might be killed, but encouraged her to remain strong and never give up her faith in Jesus. The men broke down the door, dragged Kande outside, attacked him and slashed his throat. Kande's wife Bindu, although devastated, said later, 'I will live for Jesus and die for Jesus, but I will never turn back.' That spirit is humbling.

On that shoreline, Peter was saying the same thing as Kande and Bindu. He would look the world in the eye and he would never turn back.

Several thousand Christians are killed each year because of their faith. Statistically and geographically, it's highly unlikely to happen to you and me, but the challenge to us and to them is the same: 'Do you love me?' If we do, will we love Christ enough to accept our own calling, modest as it may be, and follow him wherever it may lead?

Context is everything, but the question is the same.

To ponder

- I wonder what Peter did next, after that conversation with Jesus.
- Are you prepared to let Jesus ask you that question, 'Do you love me?'? If so, take time to hear the question and think carefully about how you want to answer it.

- When has following Christ been most challenging for you?
- Do you sense that there's a next stage in your following of Jesus? If so, do you have any intimation of what that might be, however modest?

Prayer

A is for intercession; B is more contemplative.

A As you start praying, identify who God has put on your heart at present. Take each person and visualize him or her. Then see each one being filled with the light of Christ. See them glow in the dark, full of light and joy.

B Write the names of your family and friends, and everyone in your home group or church, on strips of paper. Place them in a bowl or jar. Each day, pick out three names at random and pray for them, that they may know themselves deeply loved, strengthened and equipped by God.

A last word

In this book, we've been listening to some of the questions that Jesus asked in his ministry and then reflecting on how those questions might speak to our own faith and discipleship as well.

There's a further possibility, one that goes beyond the questions recorded in the Gospels. In the course of our own discipleship and prayer, Jesus might ask us all sorts of challenging questions that help us to make our journey more faithfully. These aren't the questions recorded in the Gospels, but the ones that come to us, for example, in our thoughts and prayers. The issue is how to recognize those questions, how to 'hear' them.

It's rare for us to hear the questions Jesus asks us in the same physical way that we hear someone talking to us. If it were as clear as that, then we'd be sure to listen! Usually, however, we hear in more subtle ways. It might be that, as we pray, read Scripture or simply reflect quietly in the presence of God, we become aware of a persistent question that needs an answer. Alternatively, it might be that we hear something in church that triggers a question which intrigues us. It might be that a friend asks us a question that won't go away. God won't overwhelm our freedom, but he'll certainly help us with our decisions.

The key factor is *recognition*. We recognize that the question we hear has a special character, that it seems to come from God. It doesn't matter, by the way, whether we think of the question as coming from God or from Jesus. We each have our own 'take' on this. The important point is that we recognize the question has a divine origin. It has an authentic feel to it. It's as if it's been there all along, just waiting to be asked.

The more pressing problem with 'hearing' Jesus' questions is how to become still and attentive enough to hear anything outside the noisy echo chamber of our own minds. There's always so much going on in our minds and so much information being pumped into them all day that we don't usually have enough interior stillness to hear a God who doesn't shout. God respects silence and doesn't demand a hearing. God is astonishingly humble and speaks quietly, as a lover does to the beloved.

I remember once having a number of opportunities for a new ministry and most of them didn't feel 'real'. However, I was then asked to apply for a major job that quite alarmed me. It felt as if God were saying, 'I know this is scary, but could this be the one?' I did as I was asked, applied and soon began to feel very much at home with the idea. I prayed, talked and listened. When I went for an interview, my instinct again told me that this would work, it was 'right'. I would have understood if someone else had been appointed but, at a deeper level, I felt sure that it was a good fit. It felt as if I was answering God's question.

It's difficult to hear God in a noisy world. What we can do, however, is nurture attentiveness to God's voice and a readiness to respond. We can begin by practising a quieter, more receptive kind of praying that attunes us to God's voice. Too often, a time of prayer can be like going on safari and crashing excitedly through the undergrowth with all the insensitivity of Westerners unused to the quiet rhythms of that environment. We catch a tantalizing glimpse of flocks and herds fleeing into the distance, but that's about all. The animals we're looking for tend to remain hidden and perhaps we begin to doubt that they're there at all. They're definitely out there, though, and what we need to do is cultivate a stillness that might encourage the animals to emerge from the undergrowth.

So, too, with the voice of God. If we create in ourselves the qualities of stillness and attentiveness, we'll come to recognize the voice, questions, promises and nudges that could take us deeper in our knowledge of God and of ourselves.

God asks us the questions that we need to address, but how we answer them is the lifelong task of discipleship – what Eugene Peterson called 'long obedience in the same direction'. As we sit quietly with God, the dust begins to settle and issues come into clearer focus. We begin to recognize the still, small voice of God and pay attention to the challenge, promise and guidance being offered.

God is a questioning God. He doesn't order us about. He invites us to discover abundant life by addressing the tantalizing questions that he leaves on the path ahead of us.

So the last word is simple.

Listen.

Acknowledgements

I'm always (or is it 'usually'?) grateful to those who ask me tricky questions. Never more so than when people read early versions of a book I'm writing and ask me why on earth I wrote particular sections in such odd ways.

For a long time, I've been wonderfully questioned in this way by a variety of kind friends. This time I particularly want to thank Alison Barr, Gordon Oliver, Michael Irving, Isobel Short and Wendy Pritchard. By means of encouragement and challenge they have markedly improved the book before you, although they can't be held responsible for its quality, nor for the inception of the project, which came solely from my desire to explore more of what it meant then, and what it means now, to take the questions of Jesus seriously.

For more years than she may care to remember, my writing efforts for SPCK have been overseen by my very skilled publisher, Alison Barr. Alison has been an ideal editor – encouraging, faithful, honest when something wasn't working, positive when it came together, feeding me ideas, holding me back from folly. I'm immensely grateful to her for her professional skill and friendship over this time.

I mentioned Gordon Oliver above, a very good friend from my days teaching practical theology and then overseeing ministry in different parts of the country. He and I have chewed over large tracts of theological and ecclesiastical territory, as well as delighting in the wonderful absurdities of life and ministry – all over splendid meals adorned with the odd gin and tonic and occasional glass of wine. I respect Gordon's heart and mind more than I can say. This may not be the book of mine that he would like dedicated to him, but that's the way it goes!

I also mentioned Michael Irving, whose friendship I have also long enjoyed from a time when he was a diocesan director of ordinands and I was trying to lead a theological college. Like Gordon, Michael holds together theology, spirituality and pastoral practice in the way I wish for all clergy, combining it with a boyish enthusiasm for the outdoors and a huge love for people. He tells wonderfully entertaining anecdotes and gets a lot of extra brownie points for his enthusiasm for my attempts at making the Christian faith accessible, interesting and inviting.

As you might have noticed at the start, I have therefore gladly dedicated this book to Alison, Gordon and Michael.

Notes

1 Dag Hammarskjöld, *Markings* (London: Faber and Faber, 1964), p. 2.
2 Joanna Cannon, *Three Things about Elsie* (London: HarperCollins, 2018), p. 69 (proofs).
3 After Michael Ipgrave, *Reflections for Every Day* (London: Church House Publishing, 2019), 5 May.
4 Brian McLaren, *The Great Spiritual Migration* (Danvers, MA: Convergent, 2016), p. 2.
5 Samuel Taylor Coleridge, Aphorism 7, *Aids to Reflection*, 1884.
6 Marilynne Robinson, *Home* (London: Virago, 2008), p. 230.
7 Sue Pickering, *Listening and Spiritual Conversation* (Norwich: Canterbury Press, 2017), p. 118
8 Mike Riddell, *Godzone* (Oxford: Lion, 1992), p. 75.
9 Sermon, quoted in Philip Yancey, *Soul Survivor* (London: Hodder & Stoughton, 2001), p. 20.
10 Lewis Carroll, *Alice's Adventures in Wonderland*.
11 David Ford, *The Shape of Living* (Norwich: Canterbury Press, 2004), p. 102.
12 John Greenleaf Whittier, hymn 'Immortal love, forever full' (1866).
13 Henri Nouwen, *Reaching Out* (New York: Doubleday, 1975), p. 52.
14 David Walker, *God's Belongers* (Abingdon: BRF, 2017).
15 Brian McLaren, 'Three Christianities', *Oneing* (Journal of the Center for Action and Contemplation, Albuquerque, New Mexico), 7(2):72.
16 Alice Walker, *The Color Purple* (London: Phoenix, 2004), p. 174.
17 Isaac Watts, hymn 'When I survey the wondrous cross', 1707.
18 Oscar Wilde, *De Profundis* (London: Methuen, 1905).
19 Lord Hailsham, *The Door Wherein I Went* (London: Collins, 1975), p. 54.
20 Tom Holland, *Dominion* (London: Little, Brown, 2019), p. 524.

21 'Jürgen Klopp – the new Liverpool manager is not hiding his Christian faith', *Christianity*, 8 October 2015.

22 Kenneth Grahame, *The Wind in the Willows* (London: Methuen, 1950), p. 11.

23 Edward Markham, 'Outwitted', *The Shoes of Happiness and Other Poems* (Garden City, New York: Doubleday, Page & Co., 1915), p. 1.

24 Richard Harries, *The Beauty and the Horror* (London: SPCK, 2016), p. 132.

25 Sam Wells, *The Nazareth Manifesto* (London: Wiley-Blackwell, 2015), pp. 28–29.

26 Julian of Norwich, *Revelations of Divine Love*, various editions, ch. 82.

27 Nadia Bolz-Weber, *Accidental Saints* (Norwich: Canterbury Press, 2015), p. 167.

28 Jonathan Sacks, *The Great Partnership* (London: Hodder & Stoughton, 2011), p. 245.

29 Martin Luther King Jnr's sermon, St Paul's Episcopal Church, Cleveland Heights, 14 May 1963.

30 Story told by John Barton, *The Church Times*, 5 June 2020.

31 David Wallace-Wells, *The Uninhabitable Earth* (Harmondsworth: Penguin, 2019).

32 Toby Ord, *The Precipice* (London: Bloomsbury, 2020).

33 Julian of Norwich, *Revelations of Divine Love*, various editions, ch. 82.

34 John V. Taylor, *The Easter God* (London: Continuum, 2003), p. 121.

35 Helen Oppenheimer, *What a Piece of Work* (Exeter: Imprint Academic, 2006).

36 Ibid.

37 Blaise Pascal, *Pensées* (Harmondsworth: Penguin, 1961), 603, on p. 222.

38 Francis Spufford, *Unapologetic* (London: Faber and Faber, 2012), p.16.

39 David Brooks, 'What suffering does', *New York Times*, 7 April 2014.

40 Quoted in Dallas Willard, *A Place for Truth* (Downers Grove, IL: IVP, 2010).

41 Barbara Ehrenreich, *Living with a Wild God* (London: Granta, 2015), p. 237.

42 Richard Harries, *The Beauty and the Horror* (London: SPCK, 2016), p. 210.

43 Vaclav Havel, in Paul Rogat Loeb, *The Impossible Will Take a Little While* (New York: Basic Books, 2004), p. 82.

44 Clayborne Carson (ed.), *The Autobiography of Martin Luther King Jnr* (London: Abacus, 2000), p. 286.